CREATING COURSES

LEARN THE FUNDAMENTAL TIPS, TRICKS, AND
STRATEGIES OF MAKING THE BEST ONLINE COURSES
TO ENGAGE STUDENTS

SELENA WATTS

392 7169

CONTENTS

ORGANIZING YOUR CONTENT CHECKLIST

This Organising Your Content Checklist includes:

- The 10 essential elements needed to organise your content so that your students can understand absorb everything easily.
- Example of a successful organisation plan that you can adapt for yourself.
- Never underestimate the power of pen and paper.

The last thing we want is for your lessons to be less than perfect because you weren't as prepared as you could have been.

To receive the Organising Your Content Checklist, simply scan the QR code below or type the following web address into your browser:

www.selenawatts.com/organising-content-checklist

INTRODUCTION: THE ART OF CREATING COURSES

"Online learning is not the next big thing, it is the now big thing."

— (ABERNATHY)

No matter what happens to the world, education will always be a big part of our lives. But in the writing of this book, we are currently at the mercy of an unknown enemy that has forced us to stay indoors. The global pandemic has changed our path, and now, we all have to adapt to the "new normal." Fortunately, when it comes to education, staying indoors doesn't have to be a problem.

As a teacher, you can continue educating students from all over the world through online teaching. Although this book will touch on the subject of online teaching, you can learn more about this in the second book of my series for teachers entitled, *Teaching Online*. If you want to brush up on your teaching skills, then you will find what you need in the first book of my series entitled, *Teaching Yourself to Teach*. In this third book, we will be focusing on the creation of online courses.

These days, online courses are becoming extremely popular. From young children to adults who want to learn new skills while they are stuck at home, there are learners all over the world. These learners are just waiting to find the best online course—and you could be one of the best people to provide such courses. Today, creating online courses isn't just a hobby, it is a booming business that you want to take part in. The best part is you don't just have to create academic online courses. These days, you can create courses that will appeal to people because they are interesting too. For instance, you can create courses in business, personal development, and even travel! Of course, you always have the option to come up with courses that focus on academic subjects like science and mathematics too.

The point that I am trying to emphasize here also happens to be the most significant benefit of learning how to create courses: superb flexibility. As a teacher, you can create courses that you have a broad knowledge in, and you can also create courses that you feel passionate about. For instance, if you are a science teacher, you can create a course or two about your specialization. After you have put your courses up for sale, then you can move on to creating courses about your passions, for instance, pet training or perhaps courses that focus on building relationships. You can also do this the other way around. Start with a course that you feel passionate about so that you will feel motivated even if you encounter some bumps in the road (after all, you will still be in the process of learning the art of course making). Then when you have practised, and you have successfully marketed your courses, you can move on with the more 'serious' and academic topics.

Even if you are currently employed as a teacher, whether in a traditional classroom setting or an online virtual classroom, you can create your courses during your free time. As you learn how to create courses in this book, you will realize that flexibility isn't the only benefit of this endeavour. In this book, you will learn everything you need to know about creating online courses. We will start with knowing your audience and deciding what type of online courses to create. Then we will move on to choosing the right niche for your courses. After that, you will learn how to find the right platform to use, and then you will discover how to start creating your own online courses. Once you are done learning the process of creation, the last things discussed in this book are pricing and selling the courses you have created.

From start to finish, this book will provide you with everything you need to start building incredible courses to share with the world. After I learned how to teach online, the idea of creating my own courses was a natural next step for me. I have been a teacher for years now, both in traditional classrooms and virtual ones. When I first started teaching, I wanted to keep improving to ensure that my students would always get the best learning experiences while in my class. With everything I have learned as a classroom teacher (through research and experience), I wrote a book about teaching.

As times changed, I realized that online teaching wasn't just a trend. It was something that we all had to learn if we wanted to become effective and versatile teachers. While online teaching made me feel frustrated and overwhelmed in the beginning, I took it as a challenge. I did my research and applied everything I learned. Apart from learning how to become a great online teacher, I was also able to write a book about this innovative teaching approach. As I said, the next step for me was to start creating online courses.

Just like you, I started my journey by learning everything that I could about how to create courses to share online by reading. However, there weren't a lot of books or online resources that provided all of the information I needed. So, I had to pour through countless articles, videos, blogs, and the like to learn everything about course building. As I was learning, I also applied what I learned. I started by creating a course I was passionate about, and when I shared it online, I saw that the course I made was well received. This motivated me to keep going. I continued creating a few more courses that were light, interesting, and fun. Then I moved on to academic courses, which required more time and effort.

Even though I am still learning, I knew that I had enough knowledge and experience to help teachers like you who want to learn how to create online courses, hence, this book. Knowledge can only take you so far, creating your online courses requires the same passion and enthusiasm that you would apply to the classroom. Being able to create your very first online course is just beyond your reach. As you learn, try to take down notes, highlight important parts, and even come up with an action plan. Each chapter represents a step in the process, and as you read each chapter, you can apply everything you have learned. If you do this, you will have created an online course by the time you reach the end of this book! Then all you have to do is check, proofread, and refine it before making it available online for interested students to purchase. If you're ready to take this journey, let's begin!

1

KNOW YOUR AUDIENCE AND TARGET MARKET

B efore you start creating courses, the first thing that you should focus on is your audience. These days, more and more schools are transitioning to online teaching. Because of the current situation our world is in, parents and students prefer to learn from home, especially since online learning has become very common. There are endless resources available online for students who want to learn new things. Besides this, teachers from different countries are learning how to teach students in virtual classrooms and so making it possible for students of all ages to continue their education from the comfort of their homes.

If you are interested in online teaching, now is the perfect time to make a move. While learning how to become an online teacher, you could also start learning how to create courses to earn some extra income. To do this, knowing your audience and target market is critical. Think about it: How will you create a course when you aren't sure who your course is meant for? By determining who your audience is, you will get a better idea of what type of course to create, what teaching methods to use, and whether your course will consist of a series of courses or a single course that includes all of the concepts. In this chapter, you will learn more about this aspect of course creation, and by the end of it, you should already have a good idea of who you want to target for the courses you will create.

MY EXPERIENCE WITH ONLINE TEACHING

Ever since I became a teacher, I have learned how to master the most effective classroom techniques to provide my students with the best learning experience. As online teaching became more popular, I worked hard to keep up with the times and learn all about online teaching. I still remember the terrifying experience of the first online class and I still look back on some of those funny memories that come out in this new teaching environment. More importantly it's the first successful teaching moment that told me I was on the right track.

Although I had experienced some challenges and struggles while learning how to become an online teacher, I was able to overcome everything while discovering new and exciting things in the process. My learning curve included understanding how to deal with students in a virtual classroom, being able to think of the right activities to engage my students, and even communicating with students effectively through various methods and platforms.

Now, I am a successful online teacher and even though I still feel more comfortable in a traditional classroom, it's easy to see the benefits of online learning and teaching. After some years, I decided to start making my own courses to teach interested students and, of course, to make a profit too. Through experience, I have realized that the first thing you must think about when creating an online course is your audience.

When I first identified my audience and target market, I found it easier to come up with a topic, create a plan, and even build outlines for my online courses. I also had a better idea of the style and tone for my courses because I knew exactly who those courses were for. During my brainstorming sessions, I thought about my target audience, and this helped me make better decisions. I even based the methods I used in teaching the different courses on my target audience. Until now, as I create more courses, this remains to be the first step in my process—and it has worked wonderfully. When it comes to your audience, you identify them first, know their goals, challenges or problems, then create a course to solve these. Then you can start marketing your course, and when your target audience discovers it, the profits will soon follow. It's that simple!

THE E-LEARNING MARKET THAT IS THRIVING GLOBALLY

Right now, the global online learning market is thriving. Because of the pandemic that has swept across the globe, e-learning has become part of the new normal. In fact, recent research has suggested that online learning will reach $325 billion by the year 2025. Imagine that! Experts also agree that this market is nowhere near saturated—it will only continue growing as time goes by.

This means that now is the perfect time to become an online teacher and to start creating—and selling—your online courses. Now that learners of different ages and people from all walks of life are turning to online courses to learn what they need. From wanting to pursue their interests, needing to learn new skills, and having the desire to further their education, people all over the world are looking for the perfect online course to help them achieve their goals.

Another important reason why the online learning market is thriving globally is convenience. Even though we are encouraged to stay at home to avoid the pandemic, online learning allows teachers to teach from the comfort of our homes. In the same way, students don't have to leave their homes to learn new things. But when you look at online learning from the perspective of making a profit, this is more beneficial for teachers. When you become an online teacher, whether you teach students in real-time or you create online courses for students to purchase, you have the potential to earn a lot of money.

No matter which part of the world you are from, you can take advantage of this booking market. You can think of this as an investment as well as a lucrative income source. By learning how to create online courses, you will be investing in yourself. And by putting your online courses up for sale, you will be giving yourself a new source of income. Of course, the more courses you can create, the more you will earn. If you manage to earn a reputation as a teacher who creates amazingly informative and engaging content, you might get followers from all over the world.

Now is the perfect time for you to start selling online courses. Since you are reading this book, you are already in the process of learning how to do this. Good for you! While it will take a lot of time and effort to create an online course, especially if you're a beginner, everything will be worth it when you are able to make your first online course available for purchase. But if you want to make a profit, you shouldn't stop there. Continue creating, launching, and marketing your online courses until you get the hang of the process. Then you can start creating courses with higher values to make sure that you are improving as an online teacher and as a course builder. Eventually, you might even get the chance to create your brand—and that's when you will have profits rolling in.

THE AMAZING BENEFITS OF ONLINE TEACHING AND E-LEARNING

As a traditional classroom teacher, you often feel like you have a lot to prove. But as an online teacher, you don't need to prove your credibility, especially if you only plan to create courses without teaching online classes. As long as you can teach in an engaging way and you can consistently provide informative content, you will gain a solid reputation in the world of online learning. This is something you should strive for because becoming a creator of online courses comes with several benefits. Here are some of the greatest advantages to look forward to:

Passive Income

If you can create amazing online courses, these would have the potential to be purchased by people all over the world even though the courses remain unchanged. Often, you would simply create a course, offer it for a price, then sit back, and watch as your course brings in money. Unless you create a course that focuses on a time-sensitive topic, you won't even have to change or upgrade the content of your course. If you have uploaded several courses online, then you can expect to receive a substantial passive income. You can continue teaching online or doing other work with the knowledge that this passive income is adding to your savings.

No matter what course you plan to make available, there will always be people interested in it. As long as you can market your course well and you deliver what you promise, people will keep coming back for more. However, if your topics tend to change over time—like if your course is about travel, parenting or topics that are currently being researched—then you may have to update your content periodically to make sure that students will continue purchasing your course even after weeks or months have passed.

Flexibility in Terms of Location and Time

If you plan to create online courses, you can work on these whenever you want. You don't have to stick to a strict schedule just to complete the course. This is an amazing benefit as it allows you to have other jobs along with your course building. For instance, if you teach at a school, you can continue creating your courses after class or on the weekends. You can even teach your courses at night, while on vacation or even at school if your employer permits you to do so. If you want to make the most of your free time, use it to create online courses. I'm a terrible insomniac, instead of counting sheep, I put the time into my courses and my new income.

Location is also flexible when creating online courses. You can create your content from home, in cafes, at school, and anywhere else you feel comfortable. You can even make your courses more engaging by filming in different locations. Or you might feel more inspired to create content while outdoors or in a new city. Unlike in a virtual classroom, you don't have to optimize the environment where you plan to create content unless you are recording a video for your course. This flexibility offered by online course-making is one of my favourite benefits as it makes me feel free and inspired.

Easy Management

Online courses have made learning more accessible to students. But they have also made teaching more accessible and manageable for teachers. Even if you're a beginner, you don't have to deal with disruptive students or behaviors since you won't be teaching in front of a class. This means that you can easily manage the flow of your lessons, you can change your methods in the middle of your course creation, and you can even create your own teaching management system to make sure that you always create high-quality content for your students.

Professional and Personal Satisfaction

There is something so satisfying about being able to complete an entire course then uploading it online for interested students to purchase. Each time you finish a course, you will get a fantastic sense of satisfaction and accomplishment from it, especially if you manage to finish a course that was more challenging than you first thought. But beyond personal satisfaction, learning how to create courses can also give you professional satisfaction. You will feel accomplished as you can continue practising your craft and while you create courses, you will also learn a lot of things along the way. As you are learning, you may even find inspiration for new courses. If you want to experience these benefits, try making a course that you aren't familiar with. If you can finish it, then you would have learned a lot and improved the different aspects of your life.

Other Benefits

As someone who has created several courses and is already earning money from them, I can tell you that this innovative teaching method will surely make you feel happier and more fulfilled as a teacher. Apart from the benefits above, here are the other advantages you can potentially experience if you put enough time and effort into creating online courses.

- Create a substantial online presence, which can help you gain more followers in the future.
- Allow you to practice your chosen craft and passion, no matter what situation you are in. For instance, because of the pandemic that the world is experiencing now, many teachers have lost their jobs. Suppose you are thrown into such a situation. In that case, you can continue teaching by creating online courses and sharing these on the right platform.
- Help you unleash your potential. For instance, if you try creating courses about topics that are unfamiliar, you might discover that you have a talent for teaching these topics. Something that you would have never discovered if you only

taught the same subjects and lessons in a traditional or online classroom.

- Add the online courses you have created and posted online to your resume. This can be a very impressive addition to your resume to give you an edge over the other applicants vying for the same position.

Creating online courses is an endless learning experience. As you apply everything you learn in this book, you will be able to kick-start your course-making journey. But as you continue creating courses, you will surely learn new things along the way. Since the online learning market is booming right now, there's no better time for you to start building unique courses and introducing these to the e-learning world.

GETTING TO KNOW YOUR AUDIENCES: THE DIFFERENT TYPES OF LEARNERS

Before you choose your niche and create the best online courses, you should first familiarize yourself with the different types of learners. In the first book of this series entitled, *Teaching Yourself to Teach*, I discussed the nine types of learners in detail so if you get the opportunity, you can read that too. For now, let's go through the four main types of learners as these will be the main types of learners you will be focusing on when creating your courses. By familiarizing yourself with these types of learners, you will be able to attract a broader audience and teach your students more effectively.

Auditory Learners

Auditory learners are the ones who respond effectively when they learn through listening. For instance, in a traditional class where a teacher stands in front and presents the lesson verbally, auditory learners will enjoy this type of set up. Often, they won't even choose to take notes because they would be listening intently to their teacher. For these learners, doing something else while listening—like taking down notes—is a distraction. Therefore, they choose to only focus on their teacher to hear everything that is said and understand the information thoroughly.

Auditory learners also love music, which is why they might play background music while studying to help them remember what they are reading. Those who play an instrument are often able to listen and replay a song. They also excel in group activities that involve verbal discussions. Whether talking or listening, auditory learners shine. While these learners do well in traditional classrooms, they might find online learning quite dreary— unless you can find ways to make things more interesting for them. If you want your course to appeal even to the most sensitive auditory learners, here are some tips for you:

- When making videos, include a lot of music to attract and maintain the attention of auditory learners.
- Include lectures in your course where you explain things verbally.
- If your online course includes short periods where you will ask the students to complete a task, include some relaxing background music to help them concentrate. For learners who find this distracting, you can simply tell them to turn the volume down until they are done with their task.
- If you can, try to hide "Easter eggs" in your video lectures. Inform your students that you will be giving them clues to discover these Easter eggs and if they find what you have hidden, you can offer a prize such as a discount for the next online course they purchase for you. This is one way you can make your lectures more fun for all types of learners, not just auditory learners.
- Incorporate verbal assessments in your courses to give these learners a chance to listen to your questions and answer them verbally too.

Kinesthetic Learners

Kinesthetic learners are the ones who respond effectively when they learn through hands-on activities and physical movement. They enjoy participating in activities and they prefer to take an active role in their learning process. Kinesthetic learners utilize all of their senses while learning. By nature, kinesthetic learners are quite active. Because of this, they aren't the best types of learners for classes that involve sitting still and simply listening to their teacher. Since kinesthetic learners are more interested in hands-on and interactive experiences, it's quite challenging to cater to their needs, especially if you're making an online course. Challenging but not impossible. Here are some tips that can help you make online courses that are engaging for kinesthetic learners:

- Include activities where your students would have to prepare things from home that they will need for the course. From lab experiments to crafts and even outdoor activities, you can make your online courses more exciting for kinesthetic learners. Of course, this depends on the nature of the subject you are planning to teach.
- You may use flashcards for certain subjects so that rote memorization becomes a more interactive experience.
- When it comes to assignments and graded assessments, give different options to your students. Don't just assign written reports or essays. Instead, give different options like creating videos, recorded speeches, or even presentations. This choice makes kinesthetic learners feel like they are involved in their learning process.

Social Learners

Social learners are the ones who respond effectively when they learn through communicating and socializing with others. Whether their communication is done verbally or non-verbally, as long as they get the chance to be with other people, these learners will thrive. Social learners enjoy doing group activities and having opportunities to discuss and interact. Therefore, in an online setting that involves one-to-one instruction, social learners might struggle because they feel lonely. As with kinesthetic learners, you have to find ways to reach out to social learners too. Here are some ways for you to do this:

- When introducing concepts or giving recorded presentations, try to be as interactive and engaging as possible. Pay close attention to things like you tone of voice and speech rate. If you can make your students feel like they are interacting with you directly, they will feel more interested in listening to what you have to say.
- Assign tasks or graded works that involve interacting with others. For instance, you can ask your students to create a survey for other people to answer. You can even ask your students to interview others as part of their research.
- Include links to forums where the students who download your course can communicate with each other and discuss what they are learning. This is also an excellent way for your students to get to know each other, especially since they are interested in learning the same things.

Visual Learners

Visual learners are the ones who respond effectively when they learn through graphic and visual presentations. While learning, they respond well to colors, charts, graphs, diagrams, and other types of visual representations. Visual learners are usually holistic and they enjoy learning as long as they are presented with visual aids. This makes them one of the easiest types of learners to teach whether in traditional or online classrooms. Since online courses involve a lot of visual aids, you won't struggle with visual learners. Still, here are some tips to help you create fantastic online courses for students who learn visually.

- When creating your content, use a lot of visual imagery, whether you are creating lessons, forums, announcements or assessments.
- Aside from giving instructions verbally, include written instructions for your students to read. You can do this when giving instructions for activities, assignments or assessments. If possible, you can even include photos to emphasize each step of the instructions.
- Allow your learners to organize their thoughts by teaching them how to colour-code outlines, create diagrams for your lessons or even make graphs to present information. Aside from learning through these visual aids, getting opportunities to create

their own visual aids will make things more interesting for them.

Depending on the types of courses you will make, you might not be able to cater to the needs of all types of learners. For instance, if your course is about history, it can be quite challenging to think of activities to engage kinesthetic learners. But with a little creativity, you can find ways to make this possible. For example, rather than giving students a time line, you can provide the information and create an assignment that involves them creating a time line. While creating content, think about these different learners (and the other types too) then try to come up with a list of activities or strategies to help them learn effectively.

DECIDING THE TYPES OF ONLINE COURSES TO CREATE

When you think of yourself as an online educator or a creator of online courses, what picture do you conjure up in your mind? Even if you have never created a course before—whether online or offline—you might have a great idea that other people will be interested in, and you can share this with them by creating a course about it. Since online courses aren't just academic in nature, you can create courses you are passionate about too. But before we go through the different types of courses to create, let's go through some of the different types of online course makers for you to determine which type you are.

Advice Giver

While you aren't necessarily an expert at certain subjects, you have knowledge and experience in different things. You are enthusiastic about learning and you want to help make other people's lives easier by giving them advice. If you're this type of person, you would be very effective at creating "How-To" or "Self-Help" courses. You can create these types of courses as a side gig to give you another source of income. This, of course, would be very easy for you as you would just be giving practical advice to others.

If you want to create courses to help other people, you should think about what type of course you will create. Broad as your knowledge is, you have to find ways to narrow down your ideas and make it easier for you to create a specific, useful, and valuable course. If needed, you can even make a series of courses on a single topic to make things more interesting for your target audience.

Expert Teacher

You are this type of course builder if you have the experience, training, and expertise in a specific subject or topic. For instance, if you are a mathematician, then you are a math expert. Therefore, you can create a course on this subject that will be truly informative and interesting. As an expert, you have the right to create courses to help others learn about the subject you are an expert in. You can create online courses to help boost your income while learning new material and inspiring others with your broad knowledge and experience.

Although you are an expert in your field, this doesn't mean that you will immediately succeed in creating online courses. If you want to succeed, research your target audience. You already know that you can provide the most informative courses. Now you should find out what challenges or problems your target audience is experiencing so that you can help them overcome those challenges through your course.

Insider Informant

This type of person is enthusiastic about a particular topic or hobby. Although you don't consider yourself an expert, you do have enough insider information about a specific hobby or topic that makes you a great source of knowledge. You may feel happy while pursuing this hobby or topic but getting the opportunity to teach others will make you feel more fulfilled. Since you also have the potential to make money in the process, this will make you feel even more motivated. Imagine how much fun it would be for you to create profitable courses about the things you feel passionate about.

As soon as you realize that you know enough about a certain topic to teach other people, you should learn all about creating courses—which is what you are doing right now. Good for you! After learning how to make courses, you should also brush up on your teaching skills, especially if you aren't a teacher by profession. The best part about this is that you can teach yourself how to teach. The first book in this series will help you learn this and make you a more effective course builder. Then you can start creating your own courses.

Professional Educator

If you are a teacher by profession, then you might fall under this type, especially if you plan to create courses that you are an expert in. As a teacher, you are already earning a living by teaching students online, offline or both. But you can earn even more by creating courses for students from other parts of the world. While staying at your current teaching job, you can learn new things and gain more knowledge by creating a series of courses to engage and appeal to different types of students. But if you are a full-time teacher, you might not have enough time to create several courses. The best thing you can do is to create high-quality courses to keep your target audience coming back for more. You could also focus on content that doesn't change frequently. Just make sure to come up with a schedule for when you will create your courses so that your students won't feel disappointed when you don't offer anything else.

To become a successful course maker, come up with a plan for it. Your income may sustain you but if you want to make a difference or create a reputation for being a professional creator of courses, you must put in the work. As long as your work isn't affected, you can continue creating courses to keep your audiences engaged in what you have to offer.

After determining what type of course creator you are, the next thing you can think about is the type of course that you will create. No matter what topic, subject or lesson you plan to teach, there will always be people willing to learn what you have to offer. This means that you can make a profit by creating courses whether you plan to go beyond your classroom and online teaching by creating an academic course or you just want to share what you're passionate about.

Affordable Paid Courses

Affordable paid online courses are the common choice of most beginners. Since you are still learning about this profitable venture and you haven't built a reputation yet, offering paid courses that are affordable will make these more appealing to your target audience. As time goes by, you will learn the ins and outs of online courses and when you have gained your own followers, that is when you can start increasing your prices. Even if you are a more seasoned course maker, you can still offer affordable paid online courses. For instance, if you create long, comprehensive courses, you can offer shorter courses related to these but at a lower price, which are more affordable and will attract more attention.

Certification Courses

If you are a professional and you have the authority to offer certifications for specific skills, you can offer certification courses. For instance, if you are an accredited Montessori teacher, you may offer certification courses to students who, after completing these courses, will receive an official certification from you. Of course, you must first make sure that you are accredited (by taking an accredited teacher certification program) so that you can give official certificates to those who take your online courses, you may be able to earn more for certified courses.

Comprehensive Courses

As the name implies, comprehensive online courses are complete and comprehensive as they will cover all related topics or lessons relevant to a specific subject or module. For instance, you can create courses on software development, digital marketing or website designing, for example. After picking your topic, you must make sure that your course contains all the possible information that your students need to learn.

Free Mini Courses

This type of course is another great option for you as a beginner. If you want to create courses that you are passionate about, you can start with mini online courses and offer these for free. Do this to give your target audience a sneak peek of what you have to offer. Just make sure that the courses you create contain high-value content. That way, the people who download your course will look forward to other courses that you will create in the future. Mini courses are very simple and they don't take much time to make. But with the right type of courses, you can use these as a springboard to launch your career.

Free Simple Text-Based Courses

Another type of free course you can create is a text-based course. These are very simple as you would only have to come up with text-based content that you will send to your students digitally. Typically, you would send the content every day or every week depending on what your students have chosen. Although this might sound easy to make, you should still make sure that all of the content you create is informative, accurate, and engaging. Because they are very simple, these courses are often offered free of charge. You can also create a text-based course to introduce your more comprehensive courses. If you can catch the attention of your target audience through these simple courses, then they might download other courses you have made right away.

Introductory Courses

An introductory course is a short preview course that you can either offer at a low price or free of charge. The main purpose of this course is to give your target audience a taste of what they can expect from you. These courses may include text-based content, coaching sessions, recorded webinars, and even live sessions. By using varied methods of introducing concepts, you can make your simple introductory course educational and engaging. These courses are also quite short and in the end, you can add a call-to-action to encourage your target audience to take the next step in their learning process by downloading other courses that you have made.

Membership Courses

You create a membership course for people who want to sign up for a subscription service to join your community. You can create this type of course if you are one of the most important members of your community, organization or group. In this course, you will talk about your community, what it's all about, and what it means to be a member. Membership courses are very useful, so you don't have to keep giving orientations to new members of your community. However, you won't profit from these unless you make a career out of creating courses for other communities or groups. If you choose to do this, you will have to work closely with the highest members of the community to ensure that you come up with the best membership course for them to use.

Mid-Range Paid Courses

These types of courses are more valuable and comprehensive than simple, affordable courses. When making a mid-range paid online course, you should go beyond the basics to provide your target audience with the information they need to achieve their goals. For instance, if you are creating a course about the Ketogenic Diet, the basic course would contain an overview of the diet along with other basic details. For the mid-range course, you would also include more valuable information such as diet tips and how to avoid the common side effects of the diet, for example. If you are a nutritionist or a health expert, this type of course would be very valuable and interesting to a lot of people.

Skill or Hobby Training Courses

These courses aren't academic. Instead, they focus on fun, engaging topics for people to learn. For instance, you can create courses about baking, painting, playing a musical instrument or even teaching English online. Think about the skills or hobbies you are very good at and try to determine how to create a course to teach them. Just make sure that by the end of your course, the students would have already learned the hobby or skill that you have taught.

Standalone Courses

Standalone courses focus on subjects that can be taught independently. You can choose a specific topic from a broad subject and create a standalone course for it. For instance, if you are a graphic designer, you can create a standalone course for Adobe Photoshop. Or if you're a teacher, you can create a standalone course for lesson planning. These topics fall within a broad subject, but they contain enough information for you to build an entire course about them.

Top-Quality Paid Courses

This type of course is the most valuable type that you can create and offer. It's a lot like a comprehensive course as it includes a lot of high-quality content to ensure that your learners have rich online experiences. When creating this course, you can include live sessions, a copy (or at least an excerpt) from a book that you have written, and you can even create a private group on a social media platform of your choice that your students can access. When creating this type of course, you would be more involved in your student's learning. After all, they will be paying a good price for your course. Therefore, you have to deliver valuable content and commitment.

Transformation Courses

This type of course is quite intensive as you would help your students achieve a specific goal. For instance, you can create a course to help your target audience learn a skill or achieve a goal by walking them through the process step-by-step. To create this course, you must be an expert on the topic. Create a list of the things you are proficient in or those you are passionate about. Then try to think of ways to help your target audience reach your level by giving them all the information they need. This type of course is also quite comprehensive, but it isn't as broad as a comprehensive or top-quality paid online course since you will be focusing on a specific topic or goal.

After determining the type of course builder you are and choosing the type of online course you will create, you can move on to the next step in your course-building process, which is to find the niche you are most comfortable with. Naturally, your income will be a main focus but don't let that lead you to create a course that isn't within your skill and knowledge range. It's better to start off smaller and build your confidence and audience.

2

CHOOSE THE RIGHT NICHE

To enjoy your course creating journey and make the most profit, you must choose the right niche. As a teacher, you would have your own experiences, knowledge, and goals, which means that the niche you will excel in isn't necessarily the same niche that I excel in.

So... how do you choose the right niche?

Although there isn't a one-size-fits-all answer to this question, there are some elements you need to have when choosing your niche. First, you should know the subject inside and out. Second, you should have plenty of experience to ensure that you create high-quality content. And third, you should be very interested in making a course on the subject. Make a list of the topics or subjects you want to use for your online course. If you have all of these three elements, then you have the potential to create a top-notch course that people will want to buy.

In this chapter, you will discover how to choose the best and most profitable niche for the online courses you will create. You will also learn the steps that you need to take before structuring and creating your course. Once you have chosen your niche, the real work can begin.

THE IMPORTANCE OF CHOOSING THE RIGHT NICHE

Do you have a fantastic idea for a course, and you can't wait to start creating it?

Good for you!

But the fact is, no matter how promising your idea is, if you don't choose the right niche to create courses for, you might not see the results you are expecting. By definition, a niche is a field of skills and knowledge that you will focus on or specialize in. The niche that you choose will define what type of content you will create and what type of learners you will cater to. You can think of a niche as a category in an online shop like eBay or Amazon. Here, your "niche" will be the category where your products will fit into.

For instance, you sell household items. This is a very broad category, and if you choose a niche that's too broad, you might get overwhelmed with all of the variations. To make things easier for you, choose a narrower category to specialize in. Going back to our online shop, your products might fall into kitchen items. Now, this is a great category to be in—it's specific but broad enough to provide variety. This is just an example to help you visualize the definition of a niche. Later, we will go through some of the best niches you can choose for your courses.

But right now, you might be thinking, "Why do I need to choose a niche? Why don't I just create courses about different topics?"

Of course, you can do this. But without a niche, it will be challenging for you to find your target audience and come up with the right type of content. Even if you have a broad knowledge of different subjects and topics, you still need to find a niche. You may focus on one niche then move on to another after you have given all that you can to the first niche. In other words, if you choose a niche right now, this doesn't mean that you can't change it anymore. In the future, when you have decided to create different types of content, all you have to do is find the right niche for it again. If you're still wondering why choosing a niche is important, here are some reasons for you:

To help you identify your target audience

When you have a niche, you can easily identify your target audience—then speak to them directly through your courses. This communication will help catch the attention of the "right people" to purchase what you have created. It becomes much easier for you to satisfy the needs of your target audience rather than trying to cater to the needs of different groups of people with different needs and interests. It is also easier for you to market the courses you create since you have aimed your course at a specific audience.

To help you find your specialization

When you have a niche, you can become a specialist in a specific area where you offer your knowledge, experience, and expertise. Even if the competition is tough in the niche you have chosen, you can still offer something great since you will focus all of your energy on very specific topics and courses. If you need to do some further investigation, you will find is simpler when your niche is concentrated. It becomes much easier for you to focus on the topics you have chosen, which allows you to create comprehensive, high-quality courses that will speak to your audience on a deeper level.

To help you stand out from the competition

When you have a niche that you are an expert in, people will notice you. It becomes much easier for you to create a personal brand and a good reputation for being an expert in the niche you have chosen. And if you can stand out, you can expect that your courses will be purchased again and again. Not only that, but you might also receive requests for specific subjects or topics from your audience. When this happens, you know that you would have already made a name for yourself in the niche of your choice.

These reasons should already encourage you to start finding the best niche for your courses. Basically, you can make things easier for yourself when you have a niche to create courses for. If you want to reach out to as many people as possible, then choosing the right niche is key.

FINDING THE RIGHT NICHE BEFORE CREATING YOUR COURSES

Suppose you already have a great idea to start with (or a couple of great ideas). In that case, you will be happy to know that there is an abundance of niches to choose from when it comes to online courses. Naturally, some of these niches are more profitable than others. For instance, due to the global pandemic that is prevalent at the time of writing, we now rely on computers and technology more than ever. Therefore, creating a course in this niche can be highly profitable.

But before you choose a niche, you must first reflect on your passions and interests. That way you can choose a niche that aligns with these. If you want to create online courses, you should already know what you have to offer. Then choosing your niche becomes much easier. To give you an idea of what's out there, here are some of the most popular, most profitable, and most enjoyable niches to choose from.

Arts and Crafts

You can create courses to unleash the creativity of people all over the world. This niche offers a wide range of audiences from artists, stay-at-home moms, freelancers, and anyone who wants to have an alternative income source that won't disrupt their day job. Plus, courses about arts and crafts are super fun to create. Suppose you have a natural artistic talent and you want others to learn how to awaken their creativity. In that case, you can create courses in this niche. And when your audience has picked up the creative skills they need, they can start their own business.

These days, e-commerce websites like Amazon, eBay, and Etsy have become hugely popular. People from all over the world have learned how to sell different types of products. From homemade crafts to beautiful artworks and everything in between, now is the right time for people to use their innate creativity to earn money. However, those who have a talent for arts and crafts don't necessarily have the know-how to start selling their creations—and this is where you come in. You can create a course to teach creative individuals just like yourself to market their unique products in the most popular e-commerce sites. In this niche, you can create courses like:

- Animation
- Calligraphy
- Carpentry
- Digital Art

- Drawing
- Fashion
- Game Design
- Graphic Design
- Interior Design
- Knitting
- Painting
- Photography
- Web Design

Business

Speaking of selling homemade products on e-commerce websites, you can go beyond this and start creating business courses. This is a fantastic niche to choose as there is a huge demand for courses that focus on monetizing hobbies. Here, your audience would already have the skills to create unique products and creations. Now, they want to learn how to sell their creations.

Combining hobbies with entrepreneurship and business is a dream for a lot of people, which is why we now see a lot of start-ups and freelancers. To learn how to launch their business, these people will look for courses that can help them out. You can be the one to provide what they need in the form of courses like:

- Advertising
- Affiliate Marketing
- All About Amazon
- Blogging

- Branding
- Content Marketing
- Digital Marketing
- Dropshipping
- E-Commerce
- Entrepreneurship and Business Basics
- Freelancing
- Search Engine Marketing
- Selling Homemade Products on Etsy and Other E-Commerce Websites
- Social Media Marketing

Career Changes or Career Development

Although we all want to pursue the career of our dreams, things don't always go as we planned. Sometimes, people need to make career changes. If they choose this path, they might not know how to do this. But if they had a course to help them out, they can start their path towards a career change to make their life better.

Of course, some people aren't looking to change their career entirely. Some just want to develop their skills to help them move forward in their career. Either way, this niche focuses on teaching people how to transition from one point to another, how to handle more responsibilities, and how to adjust to significant changes in their lives. In other words, when you choose this niche, your main aim is to help your audience find direction so that they can move forward and improve their lives. The courses you make should cater to young adults or older individuals, depending on the topic that you choose. Some examples of courses in this niche are:

- Changing Careers
- Choosing Careers
- Entrepreneurship
- Getting and Surviving Internships
- Job Interviews/Virtual Interviews
- Life Coaching
- LinkedIn and Similar Social Media Platforms
- Personal Networking
- Resume Writing
- Creating Portfolios
- Test Prep

Computer and Technology

As you know, computers and technology are very hot topics these days, which is why this niche would be an excellent choice too. Here, you would create courses that teach your audience all about the latest trends in computers and technology. Of course, to make a name for yourself in this niche, you must have the skills, knowledge, and expertise.

Creating computer and technology courses takes a lot of work, but these courses usually sell at high prices. You can cater to beginners who want to learn more about computers and technology, or you can create more comprehensive courses for those who want to specialize in a specific area. Technology has become an essential part of our lives, and you can help your audience cope by creating the right types of courses for them such as:

- Artificial Intelligence
- Building Websites
- Cell Phone Repair
- Cyber Security
- Machine Learning
- AI/AR/VR
- Gaming
- Operating Systems
- Repairing Networks and Computers
- Robotics
- Software Programming

Education

If you're a teacher, this would probably be the most obvious choice for you. Having the right qualifications to teach a specific subject or field will allow you to create a course that helps others excel as well. In this niche, you can provide educational services for specific industries along with courses that focus on educational topics too. You can create courses for traditional classroom learning, online learning, and even blended learning. You can impart knowledge of the different methods and modes of learning to help would-be teachers and other interested audiences to learn more about education.

These days, teaching isn't just for teachers. Now, it extends to anyone who has the capacity and willingness to impart knowledge. Gone are the days when we had to rely on formal education. To help others learn how to teach effectively and help students learn, you can create courses for them. You can also create courses to help your audience learn the skills they need to become capable educators. Here are some ideas for courses you can create in this niche:

- Behavioral Psychology
- Child Psychology
- Classroom Management
- Instructional Design
- Lesson Planning
- Media Training
- Presentation Skills

- Starting a Coaching Business
- Teaching English as a Second Language

Fitness and Health

This niche has become very popular as well. Here, you would create courses that focus on diets, exercise regimens, health trends, and more. People who look for courses in this niche want to learn more about certain subjects to help improve their overall health. In the Fitness and health niche don't just focus on the physical aspects. You can even create courses about mental health, psychological health, and other aspects of life. When you create courses in this niche, you have to show your audiences that you are a very reliable source or an expert in the field.

In recent years, people have become more conscious about their health. Because of this, they take a proactive stance when it comes to learning more about the most effective diets, lifestyles, and trends that they can follow. You can take advantage of this enthusiasm by creating courses to help this target audience learn what they need. But if you plan to choose this niche, prepare yourself to do a lot of research. Make sure that all of the content you include in your courses is scientifically supported, accurate, and reliable. Otherwise, you might end up gaining the opposite of the reputation you want to have. In the fitness and health niche, some examples of courses you can create are:

- Aerobic Exercises
- Aromatherapy
- Bodybuilding
- Diet and Nutrition
- Herbalism
- Martial Arts
- Meal Planning
- Mindfulness and Meditation
- Pilates
- Reflexology
- Self-Defense
- Sports
- Survival Skills
- Vegan Cooking
- Weight Loss
- Working Out at Home
- Yoga

Mathematics

Although mathematics remains a complex and intimidating subject, it is no longer as 'boring' as most people believe. These days, we apply math in virtually all aspects of our lives from managing finances, cooking, purchasing items at the supermarket, and more. Since mathematics is part of our daily lives, you should create courses to demystify this niche and provide your target audience with a more relatable and interesting way for them to learn.

Now that we are in the digital age, mathematics has become even more significant. We use various devices and online apps that often require us to know mathematics. Just make sure that the content you create won't bring your audience back to the notion that math is boring or worse, useless! When you choose this niche, you can make courses about:

- Algebra or Linear Algebra
- Calculus
- Differential Equations
- Geometry
- Probability
- Quantitative Reasoning
- Statistics
- Trigonometry

Personal Development

Beyond careers, people these days are all about personal development. Your audience here is those who struggle or get frustrated with tasks like organization, time management or even finding self-confidence. Suppose you think that you have amazing skills and you want to impart knowledge to help people develop personally. In that case, you should start right now because this is another very popular niche.

When making such courses, focus on the benefits that you can offer to your target audience. Your audience should gain high value from your courses to ensure that they keep coming back for more. Since most people feel like they don't have time to join a class to learn what they need physically, online courses are the perfect solution. They can simply download your course and learn during their free time. Here are some examples of personal development courses you can create:

- Analyzing People
- Building Self-Confidence
- Conflict Management
- Emotional Intelligence
- Goal Setting
- Investing
- Life Coaching
- Managing Anxiety
- Negotiation
- Networking
- Organization
- Overcoming Procrastination
- Presentation Skills
- Public Speaking
- Speed Reading
- Study Skills
- The Power of Persuasion
- Time Management

Relationships or Social Sciences

The courses in this niche are meant to help people enhance their communication skills and help them improve their relationships. Although many people have started 'living' in the digital world, there are those who still want to learn how to establish and strengthen connections with others in the real world. Courses in this niche can also focus on providing perspectives on how communities and societies operate.

As with some of the other niches mentioned, you have to do a lot of research when creating courses for this one. But one thing that makes this niche stand out is that you have to take a reflective approach when creating it so that your audience will learn how to reflect or ponder the points you share too. Here are a couple of examples for courses you can create in this niche:

- Critical Thinking
- Guidance and Counseling
- Research Models of Social Science
- Social Psychology
- CBT- cognitive behavioral therapy
- Religion and spiritualism

Science

As science continues to move forward, you can now present topics that we had only been visualizing in the past. This is a broad niche that you can take advantage of as people are now interested in scientific topics to learn more about our world. The methods you would use to present courses in this niche would depend on the topic you have chosen. However, just like mathematics, a lot of people believe that science is 'boring'. Suppose you want to catch the attention of your audience. In that case, the content of your courses should be interactive, relatable, and engaging. For science, you can create courses like:

- Aerospace Engineering
- Biology
- Chemistry
- Climate
- Data Science and Data Analysis
- Disease
- Environmental Science
- Genetics
- Human Physiology and Anatomy
- Marine Biology
- Microbiology
- Pathophysiology
- Physics
- Solar Energy
- Thermodynamics

Writing

Writing is both a hobby and a profession. In recent years it has evolved into something that people use to communicate, share information, and provide enlightenment to people all over the world. As writing evolved, it has become more complex too. These days, if you have excellent skills in writing, that isn't enough. You should also know how to develop content that stands out, is entirely accurate, and captures the attention of your target audience.

By choosing this niche, you can create courses for aspiring writers all over the world. Your audience here could be content writers, copywriters, editors, and even content managers. The type of content you create depends on the specific audience you are catering to. But you have to know what you are talking about to ensure that your course offers high value to whoever purchases it. Here are some examples of courses you can create for the writing niche:

- Blogging
- Book Publishing
- Book Writing
- Content Marketing
- Copywriting
- Fiction Writing
- Freelance Writing
- Podcast Creation
- Proofreading

- Search Engine Marketing
- Search Engine Optimization (SEO)
- YouTube Video Creation

These are some of the most popular niches you can choose as a beginner. Right now, these are the niches people are most interested in. If you want to make a name for yourself in the world of online courses, you can start by creating courses for one of these niches. Then if you are interested in more specialized niches, you can make your move once you have already built a strong reputation.

WAIT, THERE'S MORE! CONSIDER THESE NICHES TOO

If you have gone through the list of niches in the previous section but none of them called out to you, then you might be looking for an under the radar niche. Unlike the popular niches, these are more focused and specific. To be considered as under the radar, the niche must meet a few specific characteristics:

It must cater to a specific target audience

In other words, the niche must specifically speak to a certain group of individuals. This means that when you choose the niche, you won't have to learn more about your target audience because you would already know who you are making your courses for. If the niche is too broad and it targets different kinds of people, then it's not considered under the radar.

It must provide a specific solution for the target audience

Since you already have a specific audience in mind, then you should already know what they are looking for. When you choose the niche that caters to a specific audience, then you must come up with a specific solution to their problem. As a course creator, your aim is to help your audience by providing them with what they need. If you can do this, you can also get the assurance that your course will be highly profitable. Suppose you cannot offer a concrete and specific solution. In that case, your target audience won't be interested in your course at all.

It must have search traffic

Finally, the niche you choose should be one of the most commonly searched topics online—it should have at least a couple of thousand searches a month to be considered under the radar. By choosing such a niche, marketing your course would be a lot easier. It would be like creating content that is a hot topic—something that people are looking for.

Now that you know the characteristics of under the radar niches, you will get a better idea of what to look for. Even if you are a beginner, don't be afraid of choosing these niches if you know that you can provide the needs of the audiences that they cater to. With everything you will learn here, you will have the potential to create amazing courses. By the end of this book, you can start applying what you have learned to create courses for under the radar courses such as:

Food and Diets

This niche falls within the fitness and health niche, but it is more focused. This is one of the most popular niches right now as people all over the world are becoming more conscious about the food they eat. There are many diets for you to choose from such as keto, paleo, and vegan, for example. Then there are topics like meal planning, cookbooks for specific diets, or even cooking techniques that use a specific type of kitchen appliance like an air fryer or a slow cooker.

Try to think of a topic that involves food and diets and there will always be an audience searching for that topic. From losing weight, trying to overcome illnesses or just trying to improve their health, people are looking for specific courses within this niche that will help them solve their problems. You don't even have to be a doctor or a nutritionist to create courses for this niche. As long as you do your research, you will find everything you need. You can even create a course about a diet that you are already following. This will make your course more believable and relatable as you share your own experiences as part of the course. Some examples of courses you can create in this niche include:

- Creating Cookbooks
- Intermittent Fasting
- Ketogenic Diet
- Organic vs. Non-Organic Foods
- Paleo Diet
- Plant-Based Diets
- Popular Diet Trends
- Veganism

Home Improvement

Homeowners these days have started to realize that DIY isn't as hard as it seems. With the right knowledge, they can redecorate, renovate or improve their homes at a fraction of the cost compared to hiring professionals. Suppose you have knowledge and expertise in home improvement. In that case, you should create courses that will help homeowners complete tasks around their homes. From interior decorating to renovations and more, there are many topics you can create content for.

When making courses for this niche, you should add a lot of videos and other visual content to help your audience understand what they have to do. This is another highly sought-after niche that has grown in popularity in recent years. Here are some ideas for home improvement courses to create:

- Budget Home Improvements
- Design Trends
- Home Construction

- Home Improvement
- Interior Design
- Landscaping
- Simple Renovations
- Simple Repairs
- Home Stagging

Pet Care and Training

For pet owners , caring for a pet is a lot like being a parent. They have to discover new things, face challenges, and learn everything they need to provide the best care to their pets. If you have been caring for a specific type of pet and you consider yourself an expert, why don't you create a course in this niche? If you have experience and expertise in caring for different kinds of pets, even better!

New pet parents are always looking for resources that will help them survive pet parenting. I didn't realize how big a thing cat psychology actually was! Your course could be the resource they are looking for. However, since this niche has become very popular, expect a lot of competition. If you want to stand out, you must think of unique topics or content to offer to your audience. This will help catch your audience's attention as they browse through countless courses that focus on the same topic. Consider these unique examples in this niche:

- Caring for Reptiles
- Exotic Animal Care
- Large Pet Care

- Professional Pet Grooming
- Training Senior Dogs
- Animal psychology

Stress Management

With the current situation our world is in, stress has become an even bigger part of our lives. Unfortunately, when people don't learn how to manage their stress, they will experience several adverse consequences that will have an impact on their lives. Therefore, many people are looking for courses that can help them manage their stress levels more effectively.

To be able to create a course in this niche, you should be an expert at stress management. After all, you will be advising a particular audience. You should help them solve their problem by empowering them and enabling them to manage their situations better to avoid high-stress levels. Some examples of courses you can create for stress management are:

- Effects of Stress
- Stress Management for Business Owners
- Stress Management for Students
- Stress Management Tips and Strategies
- Types of Stress

Travel

Travel is another under the radar niche you can take advantage of. If you are well-traveled and you know all the ins and outs of traveling, you can create courses that offer tips to would-be travelers. You can even focus on specific countries and teach your audience how to survive even the most exotic locations. Here are some cool ideas for courses in this niche:

- Finding Travel Deals
- Profiting from Travel
- The Best Travel Websites
- Tourist Survival Tips
- Travel Bucket List
- Traveling on a Budget

These are just some examples of under the radar niches for you. Before choosing a niche for your online courses, think about your interests, passion, and expertise. Remember that you should have enough to offer so that the courses you provide will impress your target audience as they learn. After choosing your niche, you can start thinking of different topics or subjects for your courses— and this is when things become very interesting for you.

STEP 1: CONSIDER YOUR AUDIENCE

In the first chapter, you learned the basics of your target audience and target market. You also learned about the different types of learners. But you cannot get to know your audience fully until you have chosen your niche. To choose the right niche, you have considered your passions, interests, knowledge, and expertise. You should have chosen a niche that you feel comfortable and confident in. One that will make you feel motivated instead of overwhelmed, especially if this is your first time creating a course.

With a niche in mind, create a list of topics that you can potentially create courses for. Then you can start defining your target audience based on your expertise. When defining your target audience, be as specific as possible. For instance, if you choose the food and diet niche, your audience might be people who want to lose weight through the ketogenic diet. If you are currently following the ketogenic diet, this is an excellent course to start with. Or suppose you have chosen education as your niche. In that case, your target audience for your first course could be teachers who want to learn how to create the best and most effective lesson plans.

Defining your target audience will help you build an online course that will sell. With a specific audience in mind, you will know exactly what they need, what problem they want to solve, and even how you will market your course. If you really want to specify your target audience, you can even create a profile for your ideal student. To do this, you need to deconstruct your ideal student to help you establish the following basic information:

- Age

- Education
- Gender
- Ethnicity
- Location
- Occupation
- Goals

After establishing these factors, you will already have a basic profile of your ideal student. Then you can follow these steps:

1. Create your ideal student persona

A student persona refers to a fictional character who represents your target audience. Creating this helps you better visualize who your target market is and why you have chosen to help them out. Creating your student persona also helps you come up with a specific topic or subject that will be the main focus of your course.

2. Learn more about your ideal student (or audience)

After creating your student persona, it's time to go beyond the single person and identify your core audience. One way to do this is by learning more about your existing audience. If you are a teacher, you are already providing an audience (your students) with what they need. If you are planning to create courses, you may have a similar audience to target.

For instance, if you are a science teacher, you may choose to create science courses. In such a case, you would already have a good idea of who your target audience is as they would be similar to the students you have been teaching in your class. You can target a specific age of learners, along with all the other factors we have discussed. Compare your existing audience with the student persona of your course then try to spot any similarities and differences. This makes it easier for you to come up with strategies for how you will present your course.

3. Discover what your audience needs

Before you create your course, you should first think about what your target audience needs. Think about it: You create a comprehensive outline for your target audience and when it's time to start creating content, you realize that they don't need what you have to offer. This would be extremely frustrating for you, especially if you have put in a lot of time and effort into creating the outline of your course.

If you want to stay on track, find out what is troubling your target audience right now. Do this first. Find out what challenges they are facing or what problems they need to overcome in relation to the niche you have chosen. This allows you to include specific topics and lessons in your course that will help your target audience immensely. By doing this, you might even discover that you can create a series of courses for your target audience!

There are many ways for you to discover the needs of your target audience. You can do research, conduct surveys, join forums, and even interview people. This part of the process may take a lot of time and effort, depending on the steps you take. But suppose you already have your student persona and you have compared this with your existing target audience. In that case, this part might be a bit easier for you.

4. Learn about the competition

Now that you have a better idea of what your audience needs and how you will help them out, the next thing you must do is learn about your competition. It will be very difficult for you to choose a niche that is already highly saturated then offer the same courses or content that your competition is offering. Suppose you try to compete with course creators who already have solid reputations without offering something new. In that case, there is a very low likelihood of finding success.

Competitor research is essential as it allows you to discover overlooked areas or weaknesses that you can provide. Doing this even allows you to learn more about the niche you have chosen and the audience you are targeting. This part of the process allows you to find the best ways to make yourself stand out so that your target audience will choose your courses over the competition. An excellent tip here is to read the reviews of others who have taken the course. This will highlight what people liked and what may have been missing.

Now that you have everything that you need in terms of your audience, it's time to zone in on your target. Come up with a plan for how you will relate to your target audience to ensure that you catch—and maintain—their interest. Create a list of strategies and methods to use for your course. Then create a draft of your course's outline. With these in hand, you can move on to the next step...

STEP 2: DO YOUR RESEARCH

After a lot of thought and consideration, you should already have an idea of which niche you will make courses in along with a specific target audience. At this point, these don't have to be permanent just yet—you can still change your mind after reading this book. Armed with the knowledge you have acquired so far, it's time for you to determine if you really fit into the niche that you have chosen.

Now is the time for you to decide how you will contribute to your chosen niche. To help you do this, let's have a concrete example. For instance, you are a teacher who also happens to be a pet parent to different types of pets. Although you can start your online course-building career by creating courses about the subjects you teach (like if you are a science or English teacher), you might have more fun and you might feel more motivated if you choose to start with your passion—pet care!

Because of this passion, you have been posting on Facebook, Instagram, and other significant social media platforms, and these posts of yours are quite popular. In fact, when you go through your list of followers, you might see that people you don't know are on that list and they are actively reacting or commenting on your posts. As a pet parent, you have learned everything you need and you practice everything you have learned to make sure that your pets are always happy and well cared for.

With this kind of situation, it would make a lot of sense to create courses in the pet care and pet training niche, especially since this niche is very popular now. Since you are already experienced at caring for different types of pets and you have the required teaching skills, you have the potential to make amazing courses. In this niche, you can make courses like:

- The Ups and Downs of Pet Parenting
- How to Care for Different Types of Pets in Your Home
- Pet Safety 101
- Everything You Need to Know About Pet Reptiles (or any other pets you may have)
- Caring for Your Pets While Keeping Your Day Job

These are some examples of courses that would be highly appealing to pet parents out there. When creating these courses, prepare your social media platforms too. Make sure that people can find you on these platforms so that they can learn more about you. Think about it, if a pet parent is looking for an online course that will help them cope with pet care while managing a full-time job, your course could help them solve their problem. And when they try to learn more about you (and they will), this potential customer will see that you are, indeed, a successful pet parent—and a teacher too! This combination will immediately give you the credibility you need to gain the trust of your target audience. If you create amazing content as well, then your courses will surely become huge successes.

Of course, this is just one example of how you can start your journey of creating courses. As a teacher, you can choose to create courses about the subjects that you teach if you are more comfortable with these. If you are happy, confident, and comfortable in the niche you have chosen, you will feel more motivated to provide your target audience with incredible content.

After choosing a niche to go with, it's time for you to do more self-reflection along with some research. If the niche you have chosen is a broad one, you may want to narrow things down to make it easier for you to think of specific topics. This is where research comes in. When you have a topic in mind, go online and search for the topic on Google. This gives you a number of results and as you go through the results, take note of the following:

- Are there any sites that pop up frequently even though the titles vary? For instance, if you search "stress management," you see a site that pops up a couple of times with different topics like "Why Do You Need to Learn Stress Management?" or "The Best Stress Management Tips Ever," or "How

Stress Can Ruin Your Life." All of these topics might vary from one another, but they all come from the same site.

- When you click on different websites, do you notice a specific group of people or type of audience who are interested in the topic you have searched for?
- Do you see any similarities in terms of the information offered by different sites about the topic?
- Do you notice any trends in the types of questions being asked and answered?

These are very important questions for you to answer when doing your research. You can even visit online forums and help sites to see what your target audience is looking for and if they have any questions that remain unanswered. As you research, have a notebook or a note-taking app next to you. Use this to jot down important things you discover from your research.

By answering the questions above, you will be able to come up with unique, compelling, and valuable topics. For instance, if you see that a certain site offers a lot of information about a single topic and many people have closely followed all of the information, you can use this site as your inspiration. The website would have gained popularity because it offers comprehensive knowledge to those who need it. But what does it lack? What questions or topics can you not find on this website? If you find or think of anything, write these down.

Through your research, you will learn a lot about the type of audience interested in your topic. By digging a little deeper, you will discover things like the audience's age range, whether more men or women are interested in the topic, from which countries these people come from, what languages they speak, and even the questions they have about the topic. Finally, research allows you to see what is already offered online. You don't want to make a course that offers the same information that your audience can easily find online, free of charge. This part of your course creation process will take a lot of time and effort but if you do it well, everything will be worth it when your profits start rolling in.

3

FIND THE RIGHT PLATFORM

A s you research the best niche to choose, you should also learn more about the right platform for your online courses. Online platforms are marketplaces where you will be sharing the online courses you make—and finding the best one is of the essence. By learning about the different platforms, you can gain a lot of insights about the niche you plan to choose, the courses you plan to create, and even about your target audience.

In this chapter, we will be going through the most important questions you should ask yourself about the right platform. Answering these questions will give you a better idea of what to look for when choosing the right market. Since the e-learning market has become hugely popular right now, there are so many platforms where you can offer your courses. As a beginner, the process of choosing the right platform may seem intimidating. But if you are armed with the right knowledge, you will find the best one.

Before you choose a platform, you must first know what type, of course, you plan to offer (Chapter 2 helped you out with this). Now, it's time to learn about what platforms are available out there and which ones your courses can fit into. Aside from the niche, the platform that you choose will ultimately affect your whole process of creating courses, which is why you should find the best one. At the end of this chapter, you will even learn about some of the best platforms available now.

WHAT SKILLS DO I POSSESS? ARE THESE SKILLS ENOUGH FOR ME TO START CREATING COURSES?

First things first. If you plan to create an online course, you should start with yourself. Even if you are a teacher by profession, do you have what it takes to create content for online learners? Do you have any experience with blended or online teaching? If not, then you can learn these things from the first two books of my teaching series. The first one is entitled, *Teaching Yourself to Teach*, and this is where you can learn all about blended learning, transitioning to online teaching, and more. The second book in the series is entitled, *Teaching Online*, and this is where you will learn everything you need to become a compelling, engaging, and inspiring online teacher.

If you are already a teacher by profession, you would now have the edge over those who have the passion for creating online courses to help their target audience. If you have experience teaching in traditional classrooms, then you should also learn how to become an effective online teacher. Fortunately, this is much easier to learn when you already have previous teaching experience. To make amazing courses, you should have the following basic skills:

- You should have the ability to organize your topics or subjects into sequential and logical groups to give your students a smooth learning experience.
- You should have experience teaching students in different types of learning environments like workshops, seminars, and traditional classrooms, for example. If you have experience teaching students in online settings like webinars and virtual classrooms, even better!
- You should be prepared to adapt your communication style, teaching methods, and content to accommodate the needs of different types of learners.

If you have all of these skills, then you can easily transition into online teaching and creating online courses. However, if you lack one, two or all of these skills, then you should work on acquiring them first. The good news is that these skills are quite easy to acquire, especially if you already have teaching experience. Now, all you have to do is hone your skills and learn how to transition to online teaching.

Since you won't be able to interact with your students in the same way as you do in a traditional classroom, you might feel somewhat uninspired when creating courses. This is one of the biggest struggles beginners have when creating courses. But with practice, you will eventually get used to this kind of setup and in time, you will even start enjoying it!

WHAT TYPES OF COURSES AND CONTENT WILL I DESIGN?

The platform you choose will help you in the creation and marketing of your online courses. But before you can sign up on one of these platforms, you must decide what types of courses and content you want to design. This is important at the very beginning because the different platforms have their own guidelines for what types of courses you can share or sell on them.

We have already gone through the different types of courses in the previous chapter. By choosing one of those courses, you can start thinking about the type of content to create. For online courses, content comes in different forms. No matter what type of course you will have or what subject you will teach, you shouldn't just create a course that involves a long, endless lecture. This might be effective in traditional classrooms, but it will not work for online courses. Although there are different types of content to choose from, the process of choosing and planning should be both thoughtful and deliberate. To give you an idea, here are the basic types of content you can include in your courses:

Audio

Audio content can be valuable, especially if you want to target auditory learners. But if you want to maximize the impact of audio content, you should know when to use it. Typically, you would combine this type of content with visual presentations. For instance, if you have included a video or a PowerPoint presentation in your course, then you can add audio content in the form of narration. This is the best way to use audio content in your course.

But when it comes to adding audio content, you must make sure that you produce high-quality audio, otherwise, this will leave your students feeling frustrated. You should have the right tools to record high-quality audio and if you plan to have explanations, narrations, and discussions in your online course, make sure that your verbal delivery is clear and engaging.

Design

To have a huge impact on the learning experience of your students, you must be very careful when choosing the color scheme of your course. If you plan to make a series of courses, try to stick with a single color scheme to make this part of your brand. Choose the right combinations of colors that aren't harsh on the eyes. Also, opt for fonts that are clear, easy to read, and have the right size. When making presentations, videos or slideshows, make sure that they aren't cluttered to ensure conducive learning.

A poorly designed online course will surely create a negative impression. You know this if you have ever been on an online course yourself, for all the courses I have taken, it's been one of the deciding factors when signing up for more. If you want to advertise your course or create a short preview for it, your target audience won't feel compelled to learn more if your design isn't appealing. The design of your course should catch the attention of your target audience. That way, they can see what else you have to offer.

Imagery

Images, pictures, and other visual imagery can serve as powerful tools for learning if you can use them correctly. When adding these elements to your course, make sure that they are logically and clearly related to the rest of your content. This is not the place to add visual elements merely for show. If you do this, your learners might get the wrong idea or they might even get distracted by out-of-place images.

When it comes to learning, clean and straightforward presentations are often more effective. Unless you are creating an online course for preschool children, unnecessary elements will lower the value of your content. As you create your content, always take a moment to assess whether everything is related, meaningful, appropriate and essential. If you find any image, picture or graphic that doesn't add to the overall aim, remove it.

Video

Video content is especially effective when you want to demonstrate tasks, explain complex concepts or even give instructions. By adding videos, you are giving your students a chance to pause or even go back to the content they missed as needed. However, high-quality video content can take a lot of time, effort, and money. If you don't know how to create such content, you might even have to hire someone to do it for you so that you are sure of the type of videos you will be adding to your course.

Another thing to consider when adding video content is that videos take up a lot of space. This means that if you add a lot of video content to your course, it might take a long time for your students to download. Also, if you add too many videos, this might turn your students into passive learners, especially if your videos aren't interactive and engaging. The key to adding this type of content is to find the right balance between being interactive and informative. If you can do this, video content can be an amazing addition to your course.

Depending on the topic of your course and the lessons you have planned for the topic, you can include different types of content. This ensures that your target audience will remain interested from the start to the end.

WHO IS MY COURSE MEANT FOR?

By now, you should already know the answer to this question well. When designing a course, you should have a specific target audience in mind. Don't make the same mistake of assuming that everyone will be interested in purchasing your course. Your target audience is the group of people who will find your course most appealing. If you can identify your target audience and understand who they are, creating your course becomes much easier. Aside from this, knowing who your target audience is, allows you to create a fantastic learning experience for them. When thinking about who your course is meant for, here are some questions for you to answer:

- Who is your target market? These are the people who will most likely be interested in what you have to offer.
- What are the demographics of your target audience? This helps you understand your target market better.
- What does your target audience want to learn from your course? This will help you design the course itself.
- What types of courses are they looking for? Knowing this allows you to think of content that will help fill in the gaps in the niche you have chosen.
- How does your target audience consume content? This helps you decide whether you should create

one long, comprehensive course or a series of
short courses.

You should also consider how tech-savvy your learners
are. For instance, if your target audience is older, consider
making your course more user-friendly. That way, your
students can learn your course on their own without
having to ask help from their young family members or
friends. This is one significant thing that can help motivate your target audience and make them feel like you
have truly customized your course for them.

The type of content you choose also depends on your
target audience. For instance, if you are creating a course
for preschool children, you should use a lot of imagery.
The type of content should also suit the age of the children. Of course, it would also be helpful to add notes and
tips for the parents of your students to help them assist
their children in the learning process.

If your target audience falls in between these age ranges,
then you don't have to think of such things. In such a case,
you can focus more on understanding what they truly
want to get from your course and create high-value
content for them.

WILL I INCLUDE ASSESSMENTS AS PART OF MY COURSES?

One significant part of online courses is assessment.
However, not all courses require assessments. For

instance, if you are creating courses in niches like food and diets, pet care, and home improvement, you don't have to add assessments, unless you want to add them for fun. But if you are creating an academic course, then you should seriously consider including assessments.

Assessments are an effective and straightforward way for you to evaluate your students' understanding of your lessons. Your students will also most likely want to see the progress they have made. Since online courses are all about self-learning, you should create your assessments in such a way that your students can take the assessments on their own and evaluate their learning on their own too. You also have a system where your students can take the assessments then send them to you for evaluation. Of course, this means that you will have more involvement in your online courses—and you may offer this option if you create comprehensive or top-quality paid courses.

No matter what assessment system you plan to incorporate into your course, it would also be very helpful to add simple assessments throughout, especially at the end of each lesson. You can present these assessments in video, audio or written form depending on the type of assessment. These simple tests can come with immediate feedback to give your students an idea of how well they understood the lesson. If they don't get a good result, they may choose to go through the lesson again to gain a deeper understanding of it.

Although essential, assessments are one of the most challenging parts of designing an online course. You have to think of the type of assessments to give, a scoring or grading system, and how you will present the assessments. You should also make sure that all of the assessments you create are not only related to your content, but they will also allow your students to gauge how well they are learning.

For most courses, the choice to add assessments is entirely up to you. But if you are creating courses for your school or you are creating certification courses, then this may be a requirement. You may also offer assessments in varying difficulty levels depending on how easy or difficult your lessons are too.

WHICH TOOLS DO I NEED TO MAKE COURSES?

To answer this question, you must determine which platform to use for your online courses. As you now know, there are many of these to choose from. Some of these platforms cater exclusively to K-12 learners, some to university students, some to students looking for courses that teach practical skills, and some for corporate learning. Of course, some platforms offer flexibility as different types of audiences can use them. When it comes to tools, here are some questions for you to think about:

- Does the platform of your choice truly provide you with everything you need to start selling your courses?
- Do you need a third-party platform for hosting your video content?
- Do you need some type of shopping cart software for capturing payments?
- Do you need an email service provider to use for delivering content?
- Do you need other types of tools to make your course work smoothly?

Although the platform of your choice might help you out immensely, you should learn everything you can about the platform to ensure that you won't experience difficulties in the future. If you have chosen a platform and you realize that you need additional tools for it, find out where you can get those tools.

WHAT FEATURES SHOULD I LOOK FOR?

Before you choose which platform to use, you must understand the important factors to look for. As with any other product, finding the right features is key. With the right features, the platform you choose can either help you save time and money or help you earn money, which is one of your main goals. Here are the basic features to look for as you go through different platforms:

Analytics

As a beginner, this feature might not seem important to you. But when you start creating more courses, then you want to have the chance to keep track of your website traffic to help you understand the sales trends of your online courses. You can also opt for external tools like Google Analytics to help you find the most effective sales channels for your courses.

Custom Domains

As you build a reputation, you should consider having your own website to offer your online courses. Find a platform that offers custom domains where you can sell your courses. Beyond the customized website, you should choose one that offers security so that your customers' details will always be securely transmitted. This will make them feel safer as opposed to websites that transmit information through unsecured parts of the internet.

Direct Payments

This is another important feature for you to consider as you wouldn't want to wait for weeks or months before your customers' payments reach your account. Receiving direct payments allows you to keep track of your sales in real-time. This won't be confusing as you won't have to remember if the payments for the courses you have sold in the previous months or weeks have already reached you.

Drip Course Content

This is a convenient feature when you create long or comprehensive courses. With this feature, your students won't receive the whole course. Instead, your courses will be 'dripped' to them so that they only get portions of your content at a time. The release of this content can follow a schedule that you have already set up in the beginning.

File Type Compatibility

It would be very beneficial for you and your target audience if the platform allows you to share content with different file types. That way, you can include different types of content in your course without worrying about some of your content not working on the platform.

Mobile-Friendly

While a lot of students will access your courses using their laptops or computers, a lot of them might also use their phones to study while on the go. If you want to cater to these students, choose a platform that offers mobile-friendly formats for courses.

Unlimited Offerings

Until you launch your course and students start buying it, you won't know exactly how much you need from the platform in terms of products, storage, content, and even the number of students. If you want to avoid getting overcharged, then you should opt for a platform that features unlimited offerings. That way, you won't have to worry about looking for a new platform if you exceed your current one in some aspect.

Video Hosting

If you plan to include video content in your course (and you should!), make sure that the platform you use allows you to host videos. Although you can add external links to your courses, it's better to have the option to host videos within your courses to keep everything in one place.

AM I WILLING TO INVEST MONEY IN THE PLATFORM FROM THE START OR SHOULD I TRY FREE OPTIONS?

As a beginner, you may want to opt for a free online course platform. Although these might be simpler and offer fewer features, remember that one of your main goals is to earn money. When I wrote this book, the market for online courses is expected to grow by $21.64 billion until the year 2024, which means that now is the perfect time to create courses (E-Learning Market in US 2020 - 2024, TechNavio, 2020). But if you sign up on a platform that requires you to make payments, then you might not make much of a profit. Give free platforms a try and when you have started making good money from your courses, you may consider signing up for paid platforms.

THE BEST PLATFORMS AVAILABLE NOW

We have answered all of the basic questions about platforms for online courses. Now, the next thing for you to learn is the different platforms available right now. Here, you will learn the basics of each platform to help narrow down your options. If you feel like any of these platforms is right for you, then you can do your own research to find everything you can about it.

Academy of Mine

Academy of Mine is one of the more expensive paid platforms available as it is considered a high-end platform that offers superb customization. Here, you get unlimited hours to develop your course along with help for setting-up and launching your course with your choice of integrated customizations. Apart from helping you with the basics, one of the main goals of this platform is to help you sell the courses you make using the platform's marketing tools. Then you can keep track of your sales using the platform's analytics dashboards.

The main feature of this high-end platform is customization, you can really create a course and call it your own. No matter what niche you have chosen or what type of course you are creating, you can use the customization features of this platform to create your course from start to finish. As a beginner, Academy of Mine might be too comprehensive for you. But if you start making a lucrative business out of your course creation, then you may consider shifting to this platform to make things easier for you.

Click4Course

Click4Course is one of the newer platforms available, yet it can stand up to the well-established online course platforms out there. Its strongest features are its certificate, survey, and testing capabilities. This platform even allows you to configure the site for your students depending on their needs. If potential students want to choose one of your courses, they will be presented with a catalog. If they have already purchased one of your courses, then they will be presented with a login screen. Although paid, you can try this platform out for 30 days without having to pay a fee. It also allows you to have unlimited students, but you have to pay a certain percentage each time one of your courses is sold.

CourseCraft

CourseCraft is a unique platform as it allows you to turn your blogs into online courses. This platform is almost entirely image and text-based making it one of the easier alternatives to traditional courses. This platform is an excellent choice if you plan to create non-academic courses. This platform offers everything you need to create self-paced courses with unique designs.

CourseCraft is suitable for beginners and for more experienced course builders. Even if you don't have academic knowledge to share, you can use this platform to share your passions, earn some money, and help your target audience improve their lives. The best part is, it's super easy to use! With it, you can choose your color scheme, upload different types of content to your course, and even create a landing page. When you're done, your course will be ready for selling.

Kajabi

Kajabi is another high-end online platform that you may consider if you plan to create comprehensive online courses. This platform features automation for email marketing, robust themes for the site where you offer your courses, blogging functionality, and you can even customize your checkout process. Although somewhat expensive, you will receive a number of perks in this platform.

For the basic plan, you get a website, three pipelines, three products, unlimited emails for marketing, unlimited landing pages, 10,000 contacts, and 1,000 members. Naturally, you get more of these perks when you opt for the more expensive plans. The most powerful feature of Kajabi is its automation tools for marketing. With these, you can categorize the users in your email list, send them trigger-based emails, and even send messages with your professional brand. If you have become a master of course creation, then this can be an excellent option for you to shift to.

Learnworlds

Learnworlds is the best platform for you if you plan to create interactive courses for your students. With this platform, you get everything you need to start creating courses and selling them online while maintaining student engagement. In this platform, you can enhance your courses by adding tests, questionnaires, and other engaging content. It even allows you to customize your landing page and sales page to show off your brand.

Learnworlds has several responsive styles and templates to optimize the site of your courses along with other useful pages that offer additional information. This platform also features pre-made course catalogs. With these, all you have to do is add your content. You can even choose interesting content to add to your courses like online tests, interactive video players, e-books, and more. Your students will even enjoy the customization when they start taking your course. Marketing is easy on this platform too as you can even offer discounts and coupons to potential customers.

Openlearning

Openlearning allows you to create content for your course then teach your content through the platform. This feature allows for social engagement, which makes this platform more appealing to students. Here, you can teach academic and non-academic courses depending on what you have to offer.

You can create Short Courses that will help your students learn new skills, explore a new topic or even give a new institution a try. You can create Open Cred Courses where your students learn new skills through your practical courses that are more comprehensive than the short courses. You can also create other types of courses depending on your niche and your target audience.

Podia

Podia is another platform that is relatively new and once you visit, you will see a beautiful and appealing design. Here, you can manage your courses, students, payments, data, email subscribers, and any digital downloads right from the platform. One unique feature of this platform is that it allows you to create downloads to give them away or sell them as lead magnets. This makes it easier for you to reach out to your target audience, so they become interested in your courses.

As a course creator, you will get several options in terms of selling your online courses. You can even use this platform for marketing your courses. This is a user-friendly option as it helps you save time and optimize your workflow.

Ruzuku

Ruzuku is a platform that offers increased interaction with students thanks to its native video streaming feature. Here, you have the option to interact with your students, hold live classes, and host webinars. The platform comes with a built-in service for teleconferencing and it's also compatible with external teleconferencing services. It's a great solution if you are aiming for high levels of engagement.

While hosting these live sessions, you can incorporate the content you have made for your course. This makes the learning experience richer for your students while giving you the chance to interact with them in real-time. For students who cannot join your live sessions, they can download the recordings of your webinars from the platform too. With all of these features, it isn't surprising that you would have to pay when you sign up on this platform.

Skillshare

Skillshare allows you to provide your target audience with affordable courses making it perfect for beginners like you. This platform features a membership scheme where students have to pay a membership fee to access the different courses on the platform. However, for you, this means that you cannot control the prices of your courses. But one cool feature of this platform is the automated email system. Through this, all of the students who have signed up on this platform will potentially learn about your course through the automatic emails that they receive regularly.

You even get a referral link that gives you a bonus each time a student signs up using that link. This platform is more of a marketplace for online courses. Student members can easily search for your course using the directory. If many students review your course, it may start trending. The nature of this course makes it easy for you to build a reputation, especially if you can offer high-quality content. However, it might not be the platform for you if you want to earn a lot of money from the courses you create.

Teachable

Teachable is another paid course that offers a wide range of pricing options. If you want to get the most features and the most savings, you may want to opt for the Pro Plan. Here, you won't have to pay any transaction fees. But you can customize the completion certificates for your students, create graded quizzes, and gain access to the advanced customization options for website themes.

With this plan, you will also get support from the admin users of the platform. This is one of the most user-friendly options as it is very easy to customize your site, upload the content you have created, and interact with your students.

Thinkific

Thinkific aims to help you create an empire for your courses. This robust platform offers superb customer support, tools for email marketing, site integration for your courses (as a member), and other user-friendly features. It's another platform that offers everything you need to create your online courses and start selling them.

You can give this platform a try using their free trial that lasts for 30 days. If you like the features, then you can upgrade to the Pro Plan. This platform also offers advanced options for pricing, certificates, landing pages, and various membership bundles and levels.

Udemy

Udemy offers a fantastic student base and all of them are looking for the right courses. This platform is similar to Skillshare as it is also a marketplace for online courses. But here, the students will pay you each time they decide to take one of your courses. This means that you have some level of control when it comes to pricing your courses. However, it does come with a price range that you must stick with.

The pricing scheme for this platform is quite elaborate. For one, you will receive a higher rate from each course that you sell if the student uses your referral link. But if a student browses through the directory and decides to take one of your courses, you will receive payment for it too, but not as high as the rate you would get if the student used your referral link. This can feel quite frustrating, especially if students seldom use your referral link. If you want to get a lot of sales, then you may have to do some level of marketing too.

Uteach

Uteach is more than a platform where you can share your courses. Here, you can create a website to advertise your brand using your design and domain name. After registering on this platform, you can start introducing your courses to potential customers.

Another unique feature of Utech is its custom blog. Using this blog, you can create exciting infographics, articles, and other content related to your niche. This platform also offers fantastic customer service, which means that you can contact their team if you have any questions, clarifications or concerns.

Vedantu

Vedantu is an online platform that mainly focuses on tutoring. Here, you can host video conferences in real-time while using a whiteboard. The most popular topics in this platform are academic subjects and foreign languages. This is an innovative platform that promotes interaction with students and healthy learning with peers. It even allows you to incorporate gamification into your courses to make them more engaging.

WizIQ

WizIQ helps you come up with your courses and sell them. But just like some of the other platforms on this list, it also allows you to host virtual classes in real-time. The virtual classrooms on this platform feature several teaching tools like live chat, video streaming, whiteboards, polls, and even screen sharing. These features make the platform perfect for teachers, professors, and tutors.

Apart from your self-paced online courses, this platform allows you to teach over 200 students in a single class. This makes things more interesting for you as you get the opportunity to interact with your students instead of trying to create content for a target audience you haven't met. If you thrive on social interaction, but you still want to create online courses, this is an excellent platform for you.

Now that you know the necessary information about the different online platforms for courses, you can choose a couple of these to try out. Read reviews about the different platforms, reach out to their customer support, browse their website, and sign up for their free trials. If you can find a platform for your online course (or at least a couple of options), then you can move forward with your course creation process.

4

CREATE YOUR ONLINE COURSE

Now that you have all of the essential information you need to prepare yourself for online course creation, it's time to move on to the more practical stuff. In this chapter, we will go through the whole process of creating online courses. This should be a really important stage for you, it's like the coming together of all your hard work to create something tangible. I always get excited when I start to create my courses. Although it might sound simple enough, this process isn't as simple as choosing a topic and talking about it. You need to create a clear and concrete structure for your audiences. This ensures that they remain engaged throughout your course and they will keep coming back for more.

STEP 1: DECIDING THE GOALS AND OBJECTIVES OF YOUR ONLINE COURSE

When it comes to online courses, your goals are broad statements of what you would like your students to learn. Setting these goals provides your courses with focus, cohesion, and direction. Learning goals are the very core of course creation. During your planning stage, you have to make sure that these goals are crystal clear.

Goals and objectives are two very different things. Goals are broad, general, and achievable in the long term. However, these aren't necessarily measurable. Objectives, on the other hand, are more specific and they lead to learning outcomes right away. In other words, you can expect that your learners will be able to achieve these objectives by the end of each topic or lesson of your course. Although objectives are already quite specific, you can break them down further into learning assessments or activities to make them more measurable, realistic, and achievable.

Since goals and objectives are the heart of online courses, these should be the first things you create for your courses. Come up with broad statements about what you want your students to learn from your courses. When you have your goals, you can start breaking these down onto specific objectives that will give your learners an idea of whether or not they understood the lessons you presented in your courses. By having these goals and objectives, you can achieve the following:

- You can organize your content well to ensure that all of your learning milestones flow logically.
- You can help your learners see if their goals align with the goals you have set for your course.
- You can explain to your students your expectations to help them learn how they will evaluate themselves while taking your course.
- You can align your course goals and objectives with the assessment methods you plan to use.

Another way to look at it is this: Setting goals and objectives for your online courses helps you ensure that you are giving your students what they are looking for. When your students read these goals and objectives, they will feel better about purchasing your online course as they would see how it will help them learn what they need to learn. These goals will also help you to remain motivated and focused.

When creating course goals, write down at least three. You can come up with more as long as these goals won't make you feel confused when designing your course. To make things easier for you, think about what you plan to emphasize in your course, what are the main themes that your students will go through, and what is the big picture that you want to promote through your course.

When you have your goals, it's time to break them down into observable, measurable, concise, and specific objectives. With your goals written on a sheet of paper, have another sheet of paper ready where you will write each of your learning objectives. Make sure that these objectives target a specific aspect of your student's performance. If you want to make effective goals, you can start each of your statements with verbs. For instance, if you are creating a course about Lesson Planning, some examples of the actionable objectives you can create are:

- Understand the importance of lesson plans.
- Learn how to prepare everything your students need for lesson planning.
- Enumerate the steps needed to make lesson plans.
- Apply everything your students have learned in your course to help them create amazing lesson plans.
- Assess their understanding of your course by creating a sample lesson plan.

As you can see, these objectives are simple, easy to understand, and actionable, making them very effective. You can create one learning objective for each lesson or topic in your course or you can create a few for each. This depends on whether your topics are easy or comprehensive. Just make sure that the objectives you create are suitable for online courses.

STEP 2: BRAINSTORMING AND ORGANIZING YOUR COURSE IDEAS

With a great topic and a list of learning goals and actionable objectives, you already have what you need to start brainstorming for your online course. Take the time to sit down, focus, and have a brainstorming session to come up with all of the main topics or lessons you will teach in your course. During your brainstorming process, you can start by writing down all of the ideas that come to your mind. You can write all of these ideas down on a single sheet of paper or you can use sticky notes to write each idea separately.

It is more than likely that not everything comes to you in one session. It's amazing where your ideas can come from — a trip to the supermarket, a walk in the park, even visiting family or traveling. Use your phone to make notes of ideas that pop into your head and then add them to your brainstorming.

When you have nothing else to write down, go through your list once again. If you used sticky notes, you can simply separate the good ideas from the not-so-good ones. But if you write your ideas down on a sheet of paper, you can prepare another sheet where you write down all of your best ideas from your first list. The number of topics to include in your course depends on what type of course you plan to make and how long you want your course to be. For instance, if you're planning to create a long and comprehensive course, then you should have at least eight to ten main topics. But if you're planning to create a short and simple course, two to three main topics would be enough.

Now that you have a list of topics, the next thing you must do is determine whether these topics have high market demand. This means that the topics are highly sought after, exciting, and provide excellent value. This is where research can come in once again. After picking the main topics for your courses, search for these topics online to determine if they are in demand or not. Right now, because of how popular online learning is, expect a lot of competition. Even if you come up with unique ideas, there will still be other educators out there who will try to sell the same ideas to your target audience. While researching, try to answer the following questions:

- Are people searching for the same topics online?
- Are people talking about the topics and asking questions about them?
- Have you discovered anything missing in terms of what the competition has to offer?

By answering these questions, you will have a better idea of whether you have great topics for your online course or not. By having the best topics, you can create a bestselling online course for your target audience. Once you have your topics and you have determined their market value, do the following:

Organize your topics

When presenting your topics in your course, you should think very carefully about how to organize your topics. Make sure that your topics flow logically from one to the other to help your students learn everything they need to. Since you already have a list of amazing topics, this step is quite easy. Think about how you will present your whole course by looking at the big picture. You can even go back to your goals and learning objectives—these will help you organize your topics well. Don't be scared to go old school and use Post-it notes for each topic, you can rearrange them until you find the logical flow.

Create learning outcomes and objectives for each of these topics

Learning outcomes and objectives are essential as these will help you create the content for each of your course topics. Remember that online courses are designed for self-learning. This means that your students will have to figure out how to learn what they need by taking your courses. By including learning outcomes and objectives, your students will know what to expect.

Use measurable action words to explain what your students should expect to learn clearly. This allows them to focus on essential points in your topics, zone in on the most critical content, and assess their learning on the way. Providing your students with clear learning outcomes and objectives ensures that they will feel confident while learning your course and by the end, they will have a wonderful sense of satisfaction.

Keep things simple

No matter how complicated your course is, you should try to make things as simple as possible for your students. You may understand your course and all of the topics in it, but this isn't true for your students. After all, they would have chosen to take your course because they want to learn something of value. Suppose the topics in your courses are too complicated. In that case, your students might feel too intimidated to move on from the first topic.

By now, you already know the main goals of your course. You should have also created the individual learning objectives for each of your objectives. Now, it's time to decide that you will teach in each of those topics. For each topic, you must:

- Determine the mediums you will use to teach your lessons.
- Come up with an outline of everything you will cover in each of your main topics.
- Organize the outline of each topic so that you will start creating logical lessons instead of random thoughts just thrown together.
- Come up with catchy titles for your topics to catch the attention of your target audience.

The brainstorming process of course creation may take a lot of time and effort, but it is also the most exciting step. Here, you will start shaping your course to keep you motivated to finish it to the end.

STEP 3: CHOOSING A COURSE FORMAT

Before creating content for your online course, you have to think about the format and structure to use. In the last step, you have already organized your topics, now it's time to create a structure that your students will follow as they go through the different topics of your course. For the structure, there are several elements you must include:

1. Provide them with an **overview** of your course. This is where you outline the steps that your students will go through from start to finish.
2. Provide them with an **outline** of everything that they will learn. This prepares your students for what to expect to give them a smoother learning experience.
3. Provide them with a **reason** for why they will be learning the topics in your course. This allows them to feel good about choosing your course over the competition.
4. Provide them with **high-quality content** for each of your main topics. This helps them learn what they need to from your course.
5. Provide them with a **summary** of everything they have learned at the end of your course. This helps

connect all of the main topics with one another
and give them a better understanding of
everything they have learned.

After making sure that the structure of your course
contains all of these elements, you can decide what format
to use. Although online courses come in different formats,
some of the most effective ones are:

Week-by-Week Format

As the name implies, this format involves providing your
students with lessons, topics or content every week. For
instance, if you have a course with eight main topics, you
can release one topic a week to give your students eight
weeks to complete your topic. This type of format allows
you to teach your courses in a set amount of time. It can
also be instrumental in motivating your students to focus
on what they have to learn, especially since they have to
complete a topic within a week.

However, this format might not be very effective if your
course includes conceptual or highly technical topics. In
such cases, your students might need more time to
complete each topic and if you only give them a week,
they might get stressed. Think about the type of topics
you will be teaching in your course and determine
whether students (even beginners without any knowledge) can learn what they need to in seven days. If not,
then you may choose a different format.

Step-by-Step Format

This format is one of the most popular as it doesn't come with restrictive time limits. Here, your students have the option to take their time with each step (or topic) of your course. They will go through the topics at their own pace and when they are ready, they will move on to the next step. For this format, your students will have to finish each step to understand the next one. To pull off such a format, you need to make sure that your topics flow logically.

The step-by-step format is excellent for short and straightforward courses. But if you have more comprehensive courses, you might want to give your students some kind of time limit to keep them motivated. For instance, if you have a course with more than ten topics and you don't set a timeline for each, your students might take too long with one of the topics then lose their motivation to move forward with the remaining topics. If needed, you can consider breaking your courses into a series of mini-courses if you want to use this format. Also, make sure that the steps you create for this format are simple, easy to understand, but will provide your students with all of the information and knowledge they need to proceed to the next step.

Reference Course Format

If you don't think you can use either of the two first formats for your course, then you may choose a reference course format. Simply put, this format offers a collection of information and knowledge presented in a well-organized, logical way. You will be providing all of the content to your students and they would use it as a reference for their learning.

However, this course might not seem like a high-quality course as it won't offer a concrete structure. But if you can provide high-quality, valuable content to your students, they may see why this format makes sense for your course. If you choose this format, you should be ready to market it well so that it will still seem appealing despite its lack of concrete structure.

STEP 4: BUILDING AN OUTLINE

Before you create an outline for your course, you should have already finished all of the steps you have learned previously. If you have done this, creating an outline becomes so much simpler at this point. By now, you already have a niche, an idea for your course, the main topics to teach in your course (along with catchy titles), and a general idea of how you will be teaching these topics.

You would also have a solid structure and format for your course, which means that you have an idea of how your whole course will flow already. Now, it's time for you to come up with a specific outline for your whole course from start to finish. Here are some steps to help you do this:

Create a blank outline

Since you already have a course idea and the main topics, the first thing you need to do is create a blank outline. There are several ways for you to do this. First, you can write down your main topics on sticky notes then write down numbers below each topic. You can also create a blank outline on your computer that only contains the title (or the tentative title) of your course along with the topics. You also have the option to use a sheet of paper to create your blank outline. No matter which method you use, the important thing is to create an outline for your main topics with blank numbered or bulleted lists for each of them.

Break down each of your main topics into actionable steps

Using your blank outline, create several actionable steps for each main topic. The number of steps depends on how easy or difficult the main topic is. This is another brainstorming session that can be a lot of fun, especially if ideas start pouring in.

Think of the details of your actionable steps

Since your topics already have actionable steps, you will already have a better idea of how you will be teaching each topic. To make your content creation easier, it's essential to think of the details for these actionable steps. To do this, come up with answers for the following questions:

- What are the most critical skills you need to teach these topics and execute the actionable steps?
- What process do you plan to follow when presenting your topics and activities?
- What are the most important things your students need to learn at each step?
- How can you help your students succeed in completing these actionable steps?
- How will your students assess their learning after completing all of the steps?

By finding the answers to these questions, you will gain a deeper understanding of our course and all of its topics. This step also helps you make sure that you will incorporate all of the information you need at each step and for each topic.

Add assessments, worksheets, and other fun elements to your outline.

Although you should focus on how to present your topic and what activities to include, you can take things further by adding elements like assessments and worksheets to your outline. These supplemental materials help make your students' learning experience more effective, especially if you can place these elements into your course strategically.

As you add more details to your outline, you will start seeing everything come together. For instance, one of your main topics may include activities like video content, lectures, and even several worksheets to help your students gauge how well they have understood the topic. As you add these things to your outline, you might even get more ideas for types of content to add.

Finalize your outline

When you are done with your outline, you can start finalizing it. Depending on the method you used, you may have to rewrite or retype everything again to come up with a neat and clear outline. Instead of finalizing your outline right after you have finished it, it might be more useful to leave your outline for a few days. This gives you some time to think about what you have created and gives you a fresher perspective too.

After taking a break from the process, review your outline again and try to see if it makes sense if you have missed anything, if you have added anything unnecessary or if you have any other new ideas that may add to the overall flow of your course. Suppose you think that you have already created a winning outline. In that case, you can proceed to the next, most difficult, and most exciting step

—creating content for your course. You will be using the outline you have created for this.

One optional step that you may consider when it comes to your outline is to have someone go over it first. You can do this before finalizing your outline and creating content. Ask someone who has experience with online course-making to review your outline and give you honest feedback about it. This is an excellent way to validate your outline or even get some advice on how to improve it. After this step, then you will feel more confident about the outline you have worked hard on.

STEP 5: CREATING THE CONTENT

The final step in the process of course building is the creation of the content itself. Of course, this is the most challenging and time-consuming part of the process—but it is also the most fulfilling. Now that you have a winning outline for the topics of your course, you need to start creating the content for each activity and lesson. Content development is critical, especially since the content of your course will determine its success. With high-quality content, you will surely impress anyone who purchases your course.

Content is where you want to put most of your effort in course-making. Think about it: If you focus too much on marketing but the content of your courses isn't up to par, you will leave a lot of people feeling disappointed. On the other hand, even if you aren't able to market your course too much before putting it up for sale, if people discover that it contains high-quality, interesting content, you will still end up selling more, especially when people leave reviews about the courses you create.

If you're used to the hustle and bustle of classroom teaching, you will feel a huge change when you start making courses. You won't even be teaching in a virtual classroom. You will merely be creating different types of content with a particular audience in mind. That being said, I always imagine my class taking in my content, whether it's videos or even their reactions to worksheets . But this doesn't mean that creating content is dull or tedious. If you are interested in the topics of your course and you find ways to make these enjoyable, you will indeed have fun with the process too. When it's time for you to start creating content, here are some tips.

Do Your Research

Research is an essential part of course creation, and you even need it while creating the content itself. In fact, when it comes to the creation of content, research and planning are crucial. It will be challenging for you to create unique content if you don't come up with a plan first. Go through the outline you have made to determine if you already have everything you need, or you still need to learn some things to provide truly comprehensive content.

While researching and planning your content, unleash your creativity. If you feel like you need to add subtopics to the main content, go right ahead. You may discover that some of your topics are more interesting than others. In such a case, try to find ways to make less exciting topics more compelling. That way, you will have a well-rounded course that your students will enjoy from start to finish.

Choose the Content for Your Course and Gather What You Need

As you do your research, pick out the best type of content and ideas to use for each of your topics. It's important to keep moving forward while creating this course because this is the part where a lot of people end up stopping in their tracks. This is the part where things might feel overwhelming and if you aren't motivated enough, you might just give up! But this is also the time when your efforts will start snowballing until you complete your entire course.

With your outline on hand, write down ideas for what kind of content to use. Choose which content you will use and what type of content you will leave out. Remember— if something doesn't relate or add to the topic, you might as well leave it out. Also, make sure that each topic doesn't lack any information and you won't leave your students with unanswered questions.

Start Creating the Actual Content

Based on your outline and your research, you can now start creating the content for your course. If you followed all of the steps before this, you would already have more than enough to start working. While you might take a lot of time and effort with your first course, things will get easier the more you practice. In fact, if you have already made a lot of courses, you will even have the ability to create your future courses from scratch!

If you are a teacher, you probably have your own learning materials too. In such a case, you can use those learning materials for your online course too. Repurposing your old content is an easy way to add content to your course as long as it isn't outdated. Combine what you already have with the new content and materials you have found online to make it easier for you to fill your course with interesting content. Some examples of content you can create for your courses include:

- Articles or blog posts
- Audio files like podcasts, interviews, talks, and more
- eBooks (especially those you have written)
- Graphic designs
- HTML5 or SCORM
- Mind maps
- PDF files
- PowerPoint presentations
- Quizzes

- Videos like screencasts, webinars, recordings, and more
- Printable templates for crafts
- Games

If you want to stay on track while creating your content, you may want to create a deadline for yourself along with a schedule to meet that deadline. This will help you avoid procrastination as you will feel some level of pressure to finish your content on time. Here is a sample schedule you may create:

- Pre-production stage: 1 to 2 weeks
- Recording stage (for audio and video content): 1 to 3 months
- Writing stage (for written content): 3 to 8 weeks
- Post-production stage: 1 to 2 weeks

The length of time you need for each stage depends on what type of content you will create. Within this schedule, plot each topic you have in your course to make sure that you don't miss anything.

Determine the Most Effective and Engaging Methods of Delivery to Use

This step is part of the previous one and you will be doing it simultaneously. Since you have already done your research and you are already in the process of creating your content, you should think about the most effective and engaging methods of delivery to use. Different topics would require different methods. The same thing goes with different types of content.

For instance, if you plan to add video content, how do you plan to deliver the concepts through these videos? Will you record yourself giving discussions or will you create animated videos to explain your topic? When it comes to methods of delivery, you must find the right balance between audio, visual, and practical techniques to ensure that you accommodate all types of learners in your course.

Make Your Content Interactive

Whatever methods you use, make sure that your content is interactive and engaging. Online courses that only include long and winding discussions are too boring. You may include discussions as long as you present them well and interestingly relay them. You can even include visual aids in your discussions to make them more engaging. Another way to make your content interactive is by adding activities in each lesson. That way, your students will really focus on learning so that they can accomplish the activities you have added in the lessons.

Record, Film, and Edit Your Content as Needed

This step is part of the production stage of your content and it is usually the most time-consuming. Although possible, it will be challenging for you to create purely recorded content for your course. This will take too much time, effort, and space on your computer. Also, creating this kind of course would be quite expensive, which means that you would have to charge a higher price for it. Since you're a beginner and you haven't established a reputation yet, you might find it impossible to sell your course even though it is very interesting and comprehensive.

After recording, writing or creating your content, you must proofread and edit it first before adding it to your files. On your computer, create a folder for all of the content you create. Use the name of your course for the title of the folder then create separate folders for the main topics. Each time you finish making content for a lesson, save it in the corresponding folder. It would also be a good idea to back up your files in a separate location in case any of your files get corrupted.

If you don't know how to edit videos and add audio content, you may have to learn these skills first as part of your course creation journey. Go online and look for tutorials—you will find many of these free of charge. Also try out different video editing software because you will find some are easier to use than others. You may also opt to hire professionals, but this will cost you money. To create your own original content, there are many skills you need to acquire. You don't have to learn all of these now, but it would be helpful to learn these skills along the way. That way, the courses you create in the future will evolve and become better as you learn how to become a master course creator too.

Vary Your Content

To engage your students and motivate them to reach the end of your course, various types of content are of the essence. Each lesson must have enough information and activities to ensure that your topics are complete and comprehensive. The amount of content you include must also be manageable. If you feel like one topic contains too many lessons, divide it into subtopics. It's easier for you to hold your students' attention by providing them with short, interesting lessons than long ones that might get boring at some point.

Apart from incorporating learning activities as part of your course content, you can also share some resources that your students can use while studying. When you find such resources online while researching, take note of them and include them in your lesson. Just make sure that you won't run into any copyright issues when you add resources. To stay safe, reference your sources properly.

Before finalizing each lesson, test the content using different computers and on different browsers. This is a smart thing to do as some content might not work properly on some browsers or computers. For instance, some video formats might work fine on laptops and computers, but not on tablets and mobile phones. Or you might have created content that is compatible with Windows but not with Mac. Although this step may take a lot of time and effort, it is essential to ensure that all of your students gain access to your content without any issues. Through the testing phase, you can identify issues in your lessons so that you can fix them before you launch your course. This helps avoid any feelings of frustration when your students aren't able to move on to the next lesson or even view your content. Finally, you should also avoid making any last-minute changes to your content, especially if you have finished everything already. Since you have planned everything from the start, making such changes might have unintended effects on the rest of your course.

5

DECIDE THE PRICE OF YOUR ONLINE COURSE

After you have created your online course, the next step is to determine its price. Setting the right price can either make or break your course. As a beginner, you cannot set a very high price for your first course no matter how comprehensive you think it is. In this chapter, you will learn how to price your course appropriately. After going through the most common pricing strategies, we will answer some of the most basic and essential questions about pricing. This information will help you come up with the best price for the course you create.

PRICING CATEGORIES AND THE IMPORTANCE OF SETTING THE RIGHT PRICE

Although setting the right price for your course is another challenge for you to overcome, this is very important. You need to find the perfect price to show that your course is valuable while still making it attractive to your target audience. Before going through the different pricing strategies, here are some factors to consider when setting the price of your course:

- The value of the niche you have chosen. For instance, if your course is in one of the under-the-radar niches, you may set a higher price since these niches are in demand.
- The general pricing rule. This states that most mid-range and top-quality courses should be priced above $100. But if you are creating smaller or simpler courses, you should price them below this mark. Always remember that the prices of your courses will mirror your brand identity.
- The exclusivity of the content you offer. If you offer valuable knowledge that isn't available anywhere else, then you may set a higher price for your course even though it's your first one. Just try not to go overboard with the price.

After considering these factors, it's time to think about which pricing strategy to use. To give you an idea of your options, here are the most common pricing strategies available:

Bundle

For the bundle pricing strategy, you would offer your courses in bundles for a promotional price. If you have only made one course, you can still use this by bundling the course with another valuable item such as a short e-book or even a discount on your next course. This pricing strategy adds value to your course while making it seem more exciting to customers.

Competition-Based

For the competition-based pricing strategy, you would base the price of your course on the prices of the competition. For this, you would have to do some research to determine the best price to set. As a beginner, you may set a lower price for your course and market this as your introductory price. As you build your reputation and you gain valuable followers, then you may start increasing the prices of your courses until you reach a competitive price that reflects the true value of what you have to offer.

Dynamic

For the dynamic pricing strategy, you will have more flexibility as you base your price on the customer and market demands. If you want to change the prices of your courses over time, then you may choose this pricing strategy. However, this isn't a very common pricing strategy used in the online course market because of the nature of online courses. For instance, if you take advantage of one of the more popular niches, you don't have to change the prices of your courses over time unless you want to release a newer course and offer the older ones at a lower price. But as long as your courses remain relevant, there is no need for such a change.

Freemium

For the freemium pricing strategy, you would offer a teaser of your course for free in hopes that those who download it will choose to pay for the entire course. For instance, you can offer the first main topic of your course that explains the fundamentals of the course itself. If you can create fantastic content for this topic that will compel your target audience to purchase the rest of the course, then this strategy will work well for you.

But if your target audience isn't impressed by the sneak-peek you gave them, then you would have just given away a topic that you have worked hard to create content for. If you are interested in this pricing strategy, make sure that you can hook your audience with your freebie to encourage them to go premium. Otherwise, your time and effort would go to waste.

High-Low

The high-low pricing strategy is where you would offer your course at a high introductory price, but as time goes by, you would gradually lower the price—preferably when you have new courses to offer. This is an excellent pricing strategy to use if you plan to create a whole sequence of courses. For instance, you would offer the first course at a high price. When your second course is ready, you can lower the price of the first one and offer the second course at a high price.

This pricing strategy will work well if you can establish a good reputation right away. If you made a great impression with your first course, your target market will surely feel excited about the next one. This means that they won't hesitate to purchase at the price you set. Because of the excitement generated by your first (and second) course, new customers may choose to purchase both courses at the same time, especially since your first course already comes at a lower price.

Skimming

The skimming pricing strategy is similar to the high-low pricing strategy but with one key difference. Here, you will offer your course at a high price right away. As time goes by, you would lower the price of your course as more people purchase it, and as it loses popularity. This is a widespread pricing strategy for electronic gadgets, but you can also use it if you think you can pull it off. However, it might encourage your target audience to skip your course when it first comes out. Instead, they would wait for a few months to purchase your course when the price has already gone down.

Penetration

The penetration pricing strategy is where you would offer your course at a very low price when you first launch it and after a specific period of time, you would increase your price to make it more competitive. Naturally, if you offer a very low price in the beginning, your course will stand out against the competition.

However, suppose the majority of your target market grabs the opportunity right away. In that case, you stand to lose a lot of profits. Although this pricing strategy might work for you when you first enter the niche of your choice, it isn't ideal as a long-term strategy, especially if you want to earn money from the courses you create.

Premium

The premium pricing strategy is ideal when you have already established a reputation and your target market is eager to see what else you have to offer. Here, you would focus on the perceived value of your course instead of the actual value or the value that similar courses have on the market. This pricing strategy isn't ideal for beginners unless you are already someone famous like a celebrity or an influencer. But as an "average person", try other strategies first before you attempt using this one.

Psychological

The psychological pricing strategy is where you would use human psychology to sell your courses. There are many ways to do this. For instance, you can offer discounts or promotions with your courses. You can also offer freebies like added resources, e-books or self-help articles related to your course, for example.

Another option is to use the "9-digit effect" where you set the price of your course at a number that ends in nine. For instance, instead of selling your course at $100, you'd offer it at $99.99. Although these two prices only have a difference of one cent, customers would already see this as a great deal just because they see the number nine in the price. You can also use the designs of your marketing ads to boost your sales. If you want to learn more about this effective pricing strategy, you can go online and learn more about it. For instance, you may visit the Pricing Intelligently site as it provides a comprehensive explanation for the psychological pricing strategy.

Value-Based

The value-based pricing strategy is where you set the price of your course based on what your target market is willing to pay. To use this strategy, you would have to research the niche you have chosen to find out what is the best price for the course you have created. Although quite effective, this pricing strategy requires you to continually research to find out the best prices for your courses.

Before you choose the pricing strategy for your online courses, there are certain questions you might have. Let's go through these questions and provide the answers to make things clearer for you in terms of how to price your courses.

WHAT IS THE AVERAGE PRICE OF ONLINE COURSES?

Right now, the average price for online courses falls between $100 and $200. However, this would depend on several factors. For one, if you have created a short, non-academic course, then setting a price of $100 would be too high. On the other hand, if you have created a top-quality academic course, then setting a price of $200 would be too low even if you are a beginner.

To find out the average cost of a course in the niche you have chosen, you need to do some research. Yes, this process involves a lot of research. But the good news is that you stand to learn so much if you take this seriously. To determine the average price of courses in your niche so that you can set the right price for your own course, search for similar courses online. Unique as your course might be, there will always be other courses similar to yours. Find these courses to get an idea of how to price your courses too.

If you want to set a higher price for your courses, you should first establish your industry credibility. The more recognizable your brand is, the more you can charge your target market per course. For instance, if you are a known industry expert, then you can ask for a higher price for your courses. And if you can offer some freebies and other promotions to your target market at no extra cost, even better!

HOW MUCH DO I WANT TO MAKE FROM MY COURSE?

This is a fundamental question since you need to be very realistic when setting the price of your courses. Before you settle on a price, you must first determine if this will be your primary source of income or simply a means to generate a passive income. This is very important when setting the price.

After all, if course-making will be your main income source, then you need to make good money off of it. To do this, you must create high-quality courses and assign high prices to them. But if your courses are meant for a passive income to add to the money you earn from your job, then you won't have to focus on high prices too much. Either way, there are certain factors you can use as a guide to set a price for your course:

- If you offer courses that help your students achieve the results they need. Set a high price for when you offer a high-value course that helps improve your students' lives then set a low price

for when you are helping them achieve a simple
goal.

- If you offer comprehensive or simple courses. Set
a high price if you offer a high-value course that
includes personal coaching, online lessons,
downloadable resources, and more, then set a low
price if you offer a simpler course with minimal to
no add-ons.

- If you provide personalized support to your
students. Set a high price if you offer personalized
coaching and one-on-one interaction then set a
low price for when you only offer email support.

- If you offer the expertise and experience to create
courses in your chosen niche. Set a high price if you
possess certifications, advanced degrees, published
books, and lots of testimonials then set a low price
if you only have passion for the topic and your
course was created through self-guided research.

By looking at these factors, you can determine how much
money you can potentially make from the courses you
create.

WHO IS MY PRICING TARGET?

This is another important question because you also have
to consider your audience when setting the price for your
course. If your target audience consists of individuals who
want to learn new skills and improve their lives, you

would set a lower price. But suppose your target audience consists of businesses and corporations to provide training for their employees. In that case, you can set a higher price. Since you have already chosen a niche and you already have a specific target audience in mind, considering them becomes much easier.

HOW CAN I MAKE A PROFIT FROM MY COURSE?

First of all, you shouldn't sell yourself short when setting a price for your course. Unless you are creating a simple or short course, you shouldn't set your price below $100. Do this whether you want course building to be your main source of income or you want to use it as a passive income source. If you set a price that's too low, you might experience the following adverse consequences:

- Your target audience will perceive your course as a low-value option.
- Your target audience won't take you seriously. Generally, students know that creating a course takes a lot of work. If they see a course that's too cheap, they might not think it's any good.
- It will take longer for you to start making a profit.

Setting the right price also makes the right impression with your target audience. Aside from setting a base price for your course, there are other things you can do to make a profit from it. Here are some examples of how you can achieve this:

- Offer downloadable workbooks, assessments or activity sheets.
- Offer access to an online community where your students can discuss with other students who have downloaded your course.
- Offer personal coaching opportunities.

WHAT CAN I DO TO IMPROVE THE VALUE OF MY ONLINE COURSE (AND EVENTUALLY RAISE THE PRICE)?

With all of the time, effort, and enthusiasm you put into your course, it is definitely a valuable piece of work. But when you launch your course on the platform of your choice, it's up to your target market to decide how valuable your course is to them. After setting the right price for your course, you don't have to stop there. As valuable as your course is already, there are things you can do to increase the value of your course and potentially charge more for it. Here are some suggestions:

- Offer something unique and exciting. This will help change the perception of your target audience so that they see your course as more valuable than the competition.
- Be as specific as possible to let your target audience know that your course is the one they have been searching for online.
- Interact with your target audience in different ways. Making yourself accessible to your target

audience lets them know that they will surely get what they need from your course because you will be there to help them through it.

- Offer flexibility in terms of your pricing options. You can offer basic, upgraded, and premium versions of your courses. This allows everyone from your target audience to gain access to your course no matter how much they are willing to spend.

- Increase the value of your course by offering bonuses to make your students' learning experience more fun and satisfying.

It would also be beneficial if your course is on a platform where those who have purchased your course can leave reviews and testimonials about it. If you have a lot of these and they are mostly positive, this helps add value to your course too.

6

START SELLING YOUR ONLINE COURSE

A mazing!!! Well done. Your course is done, and you have decided on a price for it. The next and final step (for now) is to start selling your course. In this final chapter, we will be going through the best marketing strategies for online courses. While creating a course is already quite tricky, selling it takes a lot of skill too. The fact is, it takes more than just fantastic content to sell your course, especially if you have chosen a highly competitive niche. After learning the different marketing strategies, we will also go through the most common mistakes to avoid when selling your course. The information you learn here will put a perfect end to your course-creation journey. By the end of it, you will be ready to start creating and selling your very first course.

AFFILIATE MARKETING

Affiliate marketing is an exciting type of marketing strategy that involves creating professional relationships with other entities to become affiliates for each other. When you create an affiliate marketing program, this can help you grow your network and widen your reach in terms of your target audience. Each time one of your affiliates can bring customers to the platform where you sell your courses, you can offer them rewards. In the same way, you will also do promotions for your affiliate partners to get rewards from them too.

As part of your affiliate marketing strategy, you can give other people (even those who have already purchased your course) opportunities to promote your course. In exchange, you offer them rewards like discounts, freebies or in the case of business owners promoting your courses, you can offer them a certain percentage of the amount of each sale. To execute this strategy, you have to be proactive. Since you are a beginner, don't expect people and businesses to reach out to you. Instead, do your research to find out the best people or businesses that can help promote your courses to your target audience.

Some platforms will help you create an affiliate program for marketing. If you are interested in this marketing strategy, you should look out for this feature when you're trying to find the right platform to choose. As part of this marketing strategy, you should also find out who are the most influential people in the niche you have chosen.

Reach out to them and establish connections with them. Then you can ask them if they can join your affiliate program. Aside from this, here are some ways you can use affiliate marketing to your advantage:

- Writing guest posts for the personal or professional websites of the influential people in the niche you have chosen. If people see your name on these websites, they will be curious about what you have to offer.
- Reaching out to professionals who share the same goals as you. This allows you to learn from them while joining their network too.
- Interacting with the first few people who purchase your course. You can offer them bonuses, discounts or even percentages of sales if they will promote your course to the people they know.
- Attending meetups and other local events (both online and offline) that will give you a chance to meet people who have chosen the same niche as you. If you get the chance, you can even speak at such events to promote your courses.
- Hosting joint webinars with well-known people. This gives an amazing impression on your target audience as they will also see you as an expert in your niche.

Affiliate marketing is all about partnering up with the right people and working together to promote your courses. You should think of ways to encourage your affiliates to market your courses by offering them irresistible things. And when the word about your course starts to spread, you can expect a significant boost in your sales.

CONTENT MARKETING

When it comes to course creation, this is one of the most effective marketing strategies to use. Content marketing involves the use of blogs, videos, guides, and other relevant content to let your target audience learn more about your courses. This marketing strategy aims to come up with targeted content for a specific audience to generate engagement and awareness towards your brand, and the courses you have to offer.

Although highly effective, content marketing requires a lot of strategic planning to execute well. You can't just write a simple blog and expect people to feel excited about your course. These days, there are so many ways to do content marketing. And if you can find ways to customize your content, your target audience will feel even more compelled to purchase your courses. Here are some effective content marketing strategies for you to try when promoting your course to the world:

- Create a mini-course and offer it for free. This mini-course doesn't have to be too complicated, and it doesn't have to contain different types of content. Just make sure that it's exciting enough to generate interest from your target audience. You can also create a short introductory course on the main course you have made. If you offer this for free, you can entice your customers with the content you have created.

- If you have a personal blog, promote your course on it. Create an article about your course where you explain what it is all about in a fun and exciting way. You can even publish excerpts from your course on your blog to get your target audience excited about purchasing it as soon as it's available.
- Offer discounts and promotional bundles if applicable. For instance, if you have created five courses that are similar to each other, you can bundle these courses and offer them at a lower price for those who will purchase all five. Or you can also offer discounts after your customers have made their first purchase.
- Find ways to gamify your posts when promoting content. Offer challenges, polls, and even mini-games that are related to your content. This is another fun and effective way to generate interest in your course.
- Translate your course in different languages to make it more versatile. If you can speak different languages, this would be a fantastic marketing strategy as you can offer these translated versions of your courses to different people. If you cannot speak any other language, you can opt to hire a

translator to do this for you. If you find a translator who speaks multiple languages, you will be able to create a better working relationship for future projects.

- Build different types of courses then use these courses to cross-promote. When you have already created several courses, this is a fantastic strategy to use.

As you can see, all of these strategies focus on the content of your courses. Since you have created a winning course with awesome content, it makes sense to focus on this more while marketing your course. This also gives your target audience an idea of what you have to offer.

SEO MARKETING

SEO stands for "search engine optimization," and this has become extremely popular, especially in the world of marketing. SEO is a very broad subject and if you want to learn more about it, you can research it. By using SEO, you can drive traffic to the site where you are selling your courses. You do this by using specific keywords that are commonly searched on search engines. To market your course with SEO, you can create an optimized article. An optimized article would have keywords in the following:

- Page descriptions
- Page titles
- H1, H2, and H3 tags

- Images with meta descriptions
- Internal and external links
- Optimized text-based content with relevant keywords

When using keywords for SEO marketing, you should use these effectively and consistently. Your article or blog post should also have some kind of call-to-action (CTA) that will give your target audience a sense of urgency. SEO is a comprehensive marketing style. Learning how to do it is like investing in yourself and in your long-term goals.

To find the right keywords to use for SEO marketing, use online tools like BuzzSumo and Google Keyword Planner. These tools will generate relevant keywords based on the topics of your course and even the title of your course itself. When you use these keywords correctly, the site where your course is accessible will immediately turn up in the top results of Google. This is a great way to let people know that there is a course such as yours available for purchase. Although you still have a lot to learn if you're interested in SEO, here are some essential tips for you:

- When thinking of your course URL, keep it concise, simple, and relevant. Only use lowercase letters without underscores or spaces.
- Make sure to use your keywords in the titles of your marketing materials. Don't forget to add

headings and subtitles with relevant keywords
too.
- Use a meta description to describe your site and
even your course. Include your keywords
here too.
- When adding images to blog posts and articles
about your course, include an image name,
captions, and alt text.

The best part about this type of marketing strategy is that
the people who will be searching the keywords you use
will all be part of your target audience. Since they typed
the specific keywords related to your course, it means that
they're looking for something in your niche. And if you
offer what they are looking for, these people will immediately turn into your customers. If you want to learn more
about SEO marketing, do your research. This marketing
strategy might seem overwhelming and confusing at first
but if you get the hang of it, SEO can be a powerful
marketing strategy for you to spread the word about your
courses.

SOCIAL MEDIA MARKETING

These days, social media is everywhere. If you want to
learn something, you can learn it on the different social
media platforms. If something starts trending, you will
first hear about it on social media. And if people want to
find something to improve their lives, a lot of them will
turn to social media too. You should take advantage of

this fact by promoting your course on social media too. The great thing about social media marketing is that there are so many options for you to choose from. Each option comes with its own set of features as well as advantages and disadvantages. Here are some tried and tested ideas to consider if you plan to market your courses on social media:

- Start your own YouTube channel where you will introduce your course, publish updates, and even create a course promotion video for when your launch date approaches. You can also connect with other YouTubers and ask them to promote your course on their channels. Of course, you would have to do the same for them too.
- Sign up on platforms like Google Play, Stitcher or iTunes then submit podcasts about your course. Creating a podcast is a great way to let your target audience know who you are while letting them know what your course is all about.
- Create your own Facebook page exclusively for your course (this should be different from your personal Facebook profile). If you plan to make several courses, create a page for your brand where you will post everything related to your courses like advertisements, special offerings, and sneak peeks, for example. You can also take advantage of Facebook ads if you want more people to learn about your upcoming courses.
- Connect with bloggers and influencers on social

media and ask them to review your course. Offer them a discount on your course and if they enjoy it, they might even start promoting it!

- Start a group on LinkedIn and invite people from your target audience. This is an excellent option if you are targeting corporate businesses and professionals for your course.

- Take advantage of other social media platforms like Twitter and Instagram as well. The social media platform you focus your marketing efforts on would depend on the nature of your course and your marketing plans too. For instance, if you want to introduce your course through visual imagery, Instagram would be a fantastic place to do this. On the other hand, if you want people to talk about your course by sharing excerpts or quotes from your content, Twitter would be the better option.

No matter which platform you choose, you should update and optimize all of your social media profiles. That way, they all show the same information so that your target audience sees that you are invested in your marketing efforts and you aren't the type to just leave things hanging. The core concept with social media is share share and share!

AVOID THESE MISTAKES WHEN SELLING YOUR COURSE

The more you learn about marketing and selling your courses, the more you will understand this crucial process. Learning everything you can about this aspect of course creation enables you to sell your own courses online without having to rely on a third party to do this part for you. But when it comes to creating courses and selling them, there are certain mistakes you should avoid. Being aware of these mistakes will allow you to avoid them

Creating Too Much Content in a Single Course

As a beginner, you might not have the motivation or skill to create long and comprehensive courses. But as time goes by, you might feel like you want to share more with your target audience and this passion might come in a very long, comprehensive course that contains too much content.

Unfortunately, creating such a course can be a big mistake. Generally, those who are interested in taking online courses want to learn what they need quickly and efficiently. But if the courses you offer contain too much content, your students would have to take a lot of time to complete it. The good news is, it's very easy to avoid this mistake.

Suppose you have created a comprehensive course that contains all information needed for your students to

144 | CREATING COURSES

achieve their learning goals. In that case, you don't have to present everything in a single course. Go through the outline you have made and try to see where you can divide the course into smaller courses. This will give your target audience time to process each part of the course, and it even gives you time to create better content since you don't have to release everything at the same time.

The same thing goes for the actual content of your course. When presenting a topic, try to avoid adding content that takes too much time. Your students might find these too dull and they might even lose their motivation to stick with your course to the end.

Not Knowing What Methods to Use

If you are a teacher, presenting lessons may come easy to you. If you aren't a teacher by profession, but you want to create courses to earn money, then you have to learn how to teach first. When it comes to online courses, you don't need professional training to create effective and successful courses. But learning how to teach effectively and use the right methods in your online course will make it easier for you to come up with amazing content. You can teach yourself how to teach by reading the first book in my series entitled, *Teaching Yourself to Teach*. Then you can apply everything you have learned there to determine the best methods of delivery while being able to present your lessons in engaging ways.

Marketing Your Course Too Early

Creating a course takes a lot of time and effort, especially if you are a beginner. Although it might seem exciting to start marketing your course even before you have started the process of creating it, try to avoid this. Think about it: If your marketing strategies pay off and your target audience gets excited about what you have to offer, imagine how they would feel if they had to wait for months before they can download your course.

And suppose your target audience isn't impressed with what you have created after waiting so long for it. In that case, you might get a tarnished reputation. Although early marketing is beneficial for selling your courses, you must find the right timing. Start marketing your course when you're just about ready to finalize and release it. That way, you can generate interest without having to ask your target audience to wait for too long.

Ignoring Comments and Feedback

After launching your course, prepare to receive comments and feedback about it. Sometimes, customers send their feedback and comments willingly even though you don't ask them. Usually, they would reach out to you if they were either extremely impressed or extremely disappointed with your course. If you receive positive feedback, use this as motivation to start your next course. You can also post these comments and feedback on your platform for other people to see.

If you receive negative feedback, don't ignore it and try not to let such feedback bring you down. Difficult as it might be to read negative things about the course you worked so hard to build, these things can help you improve your course-making process. These comments can highlight things that you otherwise wouldn't have been aware of. Take note of all the feedback you have received and when you will make new courses, keep this feedback in mind. All improvements lead to more potential income.

Not Updating the Content of Your Courses

There is nothing like launching a course on your platform with the knowledge that people can start purchasing it. But your work doesn't end there. Depending on the nature of your course and the topics included in it, you may have to update your content regularly. Unless you only plan to offer your courses for a specific amount of time, you may have to keep updating them to make sure that the information remains accurate even if new students download your courses.

This is essential for fast-moving niches and industries like computers and technology, science, and even food and diets. If there have been any changes in information or there have been any significant updates in the niche you have chosen, make sure to update your course content too.

Not Marketing Your Course Enough

Even before you have finished your course, you should already let your target audience know that something amazing is in the works. This is where marketing strategies come in. Depending on the niche you have chosen and on your course itself, you can use the right marketing strategy to generate interest and excitement for when you finally launch your course.

If you wait too long before marketing, your target audience might be caught off guard. What's worse, they might have already purchased another course even if it isn't exactly what they were looking for. Since you didn't inform your target audience that you are about to launch the course that they are looking for, they would have chosen to look elsewhere. By using different marketing strategies, you can prepare your target audience for your launch and when you finally share your course on your platform, you will surely see the fruits of your marketing labor.

Creating Poor-Quality or Boring Content

Of course, if you create content that isn't appealing or interesting, then you can forget about making a profit from your courses. Remember that the market for online courses is highly competitive. This means that you have to find ways to stand out from the competition. The best way to do this is by varying your content. For instance, you can include the following methods:

- **Interactive videos** where your students can answer questions, reflect on the concepts presented, and engage with the videos in different ways.

- **Gamification** involves presenting your content in fun, interactive ways much like online games.
- **Storytelling** is a more animated way of presenting concepts and lessons.
- **Asking questions,** then giving your students time to reflect on these questions.
- **Sharing examples** to make your lessons more relatable and realistic.
- **Visual imagery** in the form of photos, infographics, slides, graphic designs, and other visually appealing elements.
- **Diverse assessment methods** so that your students can have fun while gauging their own learning.

Basically, anything that can make your content more interactive will also make your course more interesting. This is the final solution to one of the most common mistakes that course creators make. If you can create the best content for your students, you can get the assurance that they will keep coming back for more.

CONCLUSION: CREATE YOUR OWN COURSES NOW

The niche of your dreams is already out there. Now, all you have to do is make a choice and start the process of creating your very first online course. As I promised at the beginning of this book, I have shared with you everything you need to know about creating courses. From start to finish, this book provided you with a wealth of information to help you go beyond teaching in the classroom and provide high-value content to people all over the world.

At the beginning of this book, we started by defining the online market, knowing your audience, the benefits of creating courses, and even the different types of courses you can choose from. This chapter introduced the concept of creating courses along with online teaching. If you're interested in learning more about online teaching, you can read the second book in my series, which focuses solely on becoming an online teacher. If you feel like you need to brush up on your teaching skills and make a transition into blended learning and online teaching, you can check out the first book in my series that will help you teach yourself how to teach.

In this book, the second chapter was all about choosing the right niche. Here, you learned the importance of choosing the right niche and how to choose the right niche. In this chapter, you also learned about the most common niches available now along with some under the radar niches you can take advantage of too. The next chapter was all about finding the right platform to share and sell your online courses. As you discovered, there are so many platforms available and your choice depends on the type of courses you plan to create along with the features you need as a course creator.

Then we moved on to the steps to follow when creating an outline for your online course. A solid outline is crucial to make your content creation smoother and easier. In Chapter 4, you learned how to create the best outline to suit your needs. In Chapter 5, we discussed the steps to follow in creating your content. The content is the most important part of your online course and this is where you will put in most of your time and effort. Remember it is crucial to get the right balance of content that is both fun and highly informative. Challenging as this part might be, it is also the most fulfilling, especially if you start seeing your course coming together. The more enthusiast you are about your content, the more enthusiastic your students will be.

In the next chapter, we focused on pricing strategies. By setting the right price for your online course, you will make your creation valuable and appealing to your target market. And in the final chapter, we discussed the most effective marketing strategies you can use to start selling your course. From understanding the process of course creation to selling your courses and everything in between, this book has armed you with the information you need to find success. Now that you have all of the knowledge you need to create courses, it's time to apply what you have learned, and start making your own profitable masterpiece.

As a teacher and online content creator, I know that there are great opportunities out there for you and I feel privileged to have been on this essential journey with you. If you loved this book and you learned a lot from it, please leave a review on Amazon for all the other aspiring course creators to find this book that will help them learn what they need. Now that you have come to the end of this book, I wish you luck and I hope to see you succeed as a master creator of courses.

Thank you for reading my book Creating Courses Online. If you have enjoyed reading it perhaps you would like to leave a star rating and a review for me on Amazon? It really helps support writers like myself create more books. You can leave a review for this book by scanning the QR code below:

Thank you so much. Selena Watts

REFERENCES

Abernathy, D. J. (n.d.). *Online learning is not the next big thing; it is the now big thing.* Medium. https://medium.com/online-learning-is-not-the-next-big-thing-it-is/about

Admin. (2014, December 9). *Top 10 benefits of online teaching.* UrbanPro. https://www.urbanpro.com/online-tutoring/top-10-benefits-online-teaching

Admin. (2018, June 5). *Create better elearning courses: 8 techniques to engage your audience.* Shift. https://www.shiftelearning.com/blog/better-elearning-courses-engage-your-audience

Asanias, E. (2020). *10 ways to market your online course in 2020.* Proof Blog. https://blog.useproof.com/marketing-your-online-course

Basu, T. (2019, January 1). *55 ways to market your online course & increase sales in 2020*. Thinkific. https://www.thinkific.com/blog/55-proven-marketing-strategies-to-increase-online-course-sales/

Blackwell, J. (2019, October 7). *4 different types of online courses you can create*. Jeanine Blackwell. https://jeanineblackwell.com/4-different-types-of-online-courses-you-can-create/

Charlie, K. (2018, February 14). *5 mistakes to avoid when you create online courses*. Kev Charlie. https://www.kevcharlie.com/5-mistakes-avoid-creating-successful-online-course/

Coleman, S. (2010, August 31). *What are the benefits of teaching online?* WorldWideLearn. https://www.worldwidelearn.com/education-articles/benefits-of-teaching-online.htm

Cordiner, S. (2016, April 25). *5 deadly mistakes to avoid when creating an online course:* Sarah Cordiner. https://sarahcordiner.com/5-deadly-mistakes-to-avoid-when-creating-an-online-course/

Cordiner, S. (2017, January 4). *10 steps to creating a wildly successful online course*. Thinkific. https://www.thinkific.com/blog/10-steps-creating-successful-online-course/

Couette, M.-H. (2019, July 25). *10 most common mistakes when creating an online course*. Didacte. https://www.didacte.com/en/posts/10-most-common-mistakes-when-creating-an-online-course

Cujba, S. (2016, April 11). *10 most common mistakes in online course creation*. Raccoon Gang. https://raccoongang. com/blog/10-most-common-mistakes-online-course-creation/

Darpan, S. (2020a, March 13). *Top 7 reasons to create & sell online courses*. Spayee. https://www.spayee.com/blog/top-reasons-to-create-sell-online-courses/

Darpan, S. (2020b, March 30). *8 best niches for online courses in 2020*. Spayee. https://www.spayee.com/blog/8-best-niches-for-online-courses-in-2020/

Decker, A. (2019). *The ultimate guide to pricing strategies*. Hubspot. https://blog.hubspot.com/sales/pricing-strategy

Driver, H. (2020, January 18). *Learning styles for different types of learners*. ELearning Industry. https:// elearningindustry.com/developing-online-courses-for-different-learning-styles

Edwards, S. (2019, May 5). *Top 10 untapped niche markets in 2019 (most profitable niches)*. Online Passive Income. https://www.onlinepassiveincome101.com/reviews/top-10-untapped-niche-markets-2019/

Enfroy, A. (2020, August 1). *13+ best online course platforms (ultimate guide for 2020)*. Adam Enfroy. https://www. adamenfroy.com/best-online-course-platforms

Fernandez, M. (2020, April 10). *15 best niches for online courses in 2020 (and how to find yours)*. Persuasion Nation. https://www.persuasion-nation.com/blog/15-best-niches-for-online-courses-in-2019-and-how-to-find-yours

Ferriman, J. (2019, July 23). *15 online course niches that make money.* LearnDash. https://www.learndash.com/15-online-course-niches-that-make-money/

Flynn, P. (2020). *The top 11 mistakes to avoid when creating and marketing an online course.* Smart Passive Income. https://www.smartpassiveincome.com/guide/spis-essential-guide-to-online-courses/online-course-mistakes/

Gani, F. (2018, September 13). *The 9 best platforms to create and sell online courses.* Zapier. https://zapier.com/blog/online-course-platforms/

Garst, K. (2019, February 25). *The complete guide on how to price your online course for the greatest success.* Kim Garst. https://kimgarst.com/how-to-price-your-online-course/

Ghosh, S. (2017, August 16). *3 reasons why it's important to have a niche in your business.* Chelsea Krost. https://chelseakrost.com/3-reasons-important-niche-business/

Glendinning, J. (2019, August 8). *How to price your online course: Essential lessons from 9 years of course building.* Mirasee. https://mirasee.com/blog/online-course-pricing/#The_Perks_of_Proper_Pricing

Gregory, C. (2018, January 8). *Top 10 benefits of creating online courses for fashion tutors.* We Teach Fashion. https://

www.weteachfashion.com/blog/why-every-tutor-should-create-an-online-course

Guest Contributor. (2017a, June 6). *5 keys to picking the right online course platform for your business.* Thinkific. https://www.thinkific.com/blog/picking-online-course-platform/

Guest Contributor. (2017b, June 27). *5 questions to ask yourself before you create an online course.* Thinkific. https://www.thinkific.com/blog/questions-before-create-online-course/

Gutierrez, K. (2017, August 8). *Proactive elearning design: 10 essential questions you should ask before starting.* SHIFT. https://www.shiftelearning.com/blog/essential-questions-before-starting-elearning

Hockney, A. (2016, March 24). *13 cheap & easy methods to market your course with online communities.* Teachable. https://teachable.com/blog/13-cheap-easy-methods-to-market-your-course-with-online-communities

Iny, D. (2016, August 16). *4 types of online course creators: Which one are you?* Teachable. https://teachable.com/blog/4-types-of-online-course-creators-which-one-are-you

Johnson, N. (2016, July 15). *10 proven strategies for marketing your online course.* Fly Plugins. https://flyplugins.com/10-proven-strategies-marketing-online-course/

Kajabi Heroes. (2019, June 6). *The top 10 most profitable under the radar niches for ecourses.* Kajabi. https://kajabi.

com/blog/the-top-10-most-profitable-under-the-radar-niches-for-e-courses

Kajabi Team. (2018, July 17). *6 ideas to help you brainstorm your online course.* Kajabi. https://kajabi.com/blog/6-online-course-brainstorm-ideas

Kelly, R. (2015, January 16). *Six tips for preparing your online course.* Faculty Focus. https://www.facultyfocus.com/articles/online-education/six-tips-preparing-online-course/

Kokoulina, O. (2020, March 13). *How to pick a niche for your online courses.* Flora Blog. https://www.floralms.com/blog/how-to-pick-a-niche-for-your-online-courses

Laithangbam, M. (2020, February 28). *Online course platforms: How to choose the right one.* ProProfs Learning. https://www.proprofs.com/c/lms/complete-guide-choosing-best-online-course-platform/

Laja, P. (2019, August 11). *How to identify your online target audience and sell more.* CXL. https://cxl.com/blog/how-to-identify-your-online-target-audience/

Lievers, M. (2015, December 10). *How to choose a fail-proof online course topic.* Thinkific. https://www.thinkific.com/blog/choose-online-course-topic/

Malekos, N. (2019a, April 10). *How to price an online course | LearnWorlds blog.* LearnWorlds. https://www.learnworlds.com/pricing-online-courses-ultimate-guide/

Malekos, N. (2019b, November 28). *How much money can you make selling online courses?* LearnWorlds. https://www.learnworlds.com/how-much-money-can-you-make-selling-online-courses/

Malekos, N., & Papadopoulou, A. (2019, December 6). *How to create an online course in 2020.* LearnWorlds. https://www.learnworlds.com/how-to-create-an-online-course/#design

Markidan, L. (2018a, June 11). *16 fool-proof marketing strategies for online courses.* Podia. https://www.podia.com/articles/online-course-marketing-strategies

Markidan, L. (2018b, September 18). *How much should you charge for your online course?* Podia. https://www.podia.com/articles/how-much-should-you-charge-for-your-online-course

Mirzoyan, V. (2020, May 25). *8 best online teaching sites that will inspire you.* AIST Global. https://aist.global/en/seven-best-online-teaching-sites-that-will-inspire-you

Murphy, S. (2015, October 27). *Developing online learning content: Ask these questions first.* LearnUpon. https://www.learnupon.com/blog/developing-online-learning-content-ask-these-questions-first/

Nicholson, C. (2018, June 7). *How to structure the lesson of your online course.* The Course Whisperer. https://www.thecoursewhisperer.co/how-to-structure-the-lesson-of-your-online-course/

Online Course Coach. (2017, February 28). *5 types of online courses a speaker can create.* Online Course Coach. https://onlinecoursecoach.com/5-types-of-online-courses-a-speaker-can-create/

Otero, Á. (2019, January 31). *The 6 common mistakes when creating your online course.* IsEazy Blog. https://iseazy.com/blog/en/the-6-common-mistakes-when-creating-your-online-course/

Papadopoulou, A. (2019, February 14). *Learning goals and objectives in course design.* LearnWorlds. https://www.learnworlds.com/learning-goals-objectives/

Papadopoulou, A. (2020, March 24). *How to teach online & earn money in 2020: Definitive guide.* LearnWorlds. https://www.learnworlds.com/how-to-teach-online/

Petrick, D. (n.d.). *4 things to consider when choosing an online platform that's right for you.* Wiley. https://www.wiley.com/network/instructors-students/teaching-strategies/4-things-to-consider-when-choosing-an-online-platform-thats-right-for-you

Podia Team. (n.d.). *A buyer's guide for choosing the best online course platform for you.* Podia. https://www.podia.com/online-course-platform-buyers-guide

Pumphrey, A. (2017, July 19). *How to create a clear & engaging online course outline | Issue 07 | Online courses.* ConvertKit. https://convertkit.com/online-course-outline

Raouna, K. (2019, July 2). *30 ideas to help you promote your online course to students.* LearnWorlds. https://www. learnworlds.com/30-marketing-ideas-promote-online-course/

Reclam, R. (2018, July 18). *How to outline your online course.* Rachel Reclam. https://www.rachelreclam.com/blog/ 2018/7/18/how-to-outline-your-online-course

Sanders, K. (2020). *9 ways to use social media to promote your online course.* Post Planner. https://www.postplanner.com/ blog/9-ways-to-use-social-media-promote-online-course

Sayers, K. (2020, May 13). *Where should you teach online classes? 4 popular platforms.* Mompreneur Money. https:// www.mompreneurmoney.com/where-should-you-teach-online/

Sayner, A. (2020, February 25). *How to structure & outline your online course.* Online Course How. https://www. onlinecoursehow.com/tips/online-course-structure/

Shivler, K. (n.d.). *Creating course content.* How to Build an Online Course. https://howtobuildanonlinecourse.com/ creating-course-content/

TechNavio. (2020, July). *E-Learning Market in US 2020-2024.* Market Research. https://www.marketresearch. com/Infiniti-Research-Limited-v2680/Learning-13479374/

Timm, M. (2018, March 20). *How to find an audience for your online course*. Teachable. https://teachable.com/blog/find-audience

Tsouvalas, J. (2018, August 1). *Search engine optimization for online courses: A beginners' guide*. LearnWorlds. https://www.learnworlds.com/search-engine-optimization-online-courses-beginners-guide/

University of Kansas. (2019, July 31). *Application deadline: Spring 2020*. Ku.Edu. https://educationonline.ku.edu/community/4-different-learning-styles-to-know

Weiss, M. (2019). *A simple formula for attracting the right audience to your online course*. Client Engagement Academy. https://www.clientengagementacademy.com/blog/formula-target-audience-sell-online-courses/

Yesil, D. (2016, September 2). *8 online teaching platforms that will make you want to teach online*. Medium. https://medium.com/@didolores/8-online-teaching-platforms-that-will-make-you-want-to-teach-online-1b9b23dc2503

Made in the USA
Coppell, TX
03 May 2021